PUBLICATIONS OF THE SCOTTISH COUNCIL FOR
RESEARCH IN EDUCATION

XXX

THE TREND OF SCOTTISH INTELLIGENCE

A COMPARISON OF THE
1947 AND 1932 SURVEYS OF THE INTELLIGENCE
OF ELEVEN-YEAR-OLD PUPILS

THE TREND OF SCOTTISH INTELLIGENCE

A COMPARISON OF THE
1947 AND 1932 SURVEYS OF THE INTELLIGENCE
OF ELEVEN-YEAR-OLD PUPILS

SPONSORED BY
THE POPULATION INVESTIGATION COMMITTEE
AND
THE SCOTTISH COUNCIL FOR RESEARCH IN EDUCATION

UNIVERSITY OF LONDON PRESS LTD.
WARWICK SQUARE, LONDON, E.C. 4.
1949

Printed in Great Britain by
ROBERT CUNNINGHAM & SONS LTD., ALVA

MENTAL SURVEY COMMITTEE

Chairman
GODFREY H. THOMSON, D.C.L., D.Sc., Ph.D., F.E.I.S. (Hon.), F.R.S.E., Professor of Education, University of Edinburgh

A. C. AITKEN, F.R.S., F.R.S.E., M.A., D.Sc., Professor of Mathematics, University of Edinburgh

D. V. GLASS, B.Sc. (Econ.), Ph.D., Professor of Sociology, London School of Economics and Political Science

D. KENNEDY-FRASER, M.A., B.Sc., F.R.S.E., Jordanhill Training College, Glasgow

D. N. LAWLEY, M.A., D.Sc., Department of Mathematics, University of Edinburgh

D. M. McINTOSH, M.A., B.Sc., B.Ed., Ph.D., F.R.S.E., F.E.I.S., Director of Education, Fife Education Committee

W. L. McKINLAY, M.A., B.Sc., F.E.I.S., The Mount School, Greenock

J. MAXWELL, M.A., B.Ed., Moray House Training College, Edinburgh

A. M. ORR, M.A., B.Sc., F.E.I.S., Rothesay Public School, Rothesay

J. A. FRASER ROBERTS, M.A., M.D., D.Sc., F.R.C.P., F.R.S.E., Burden Mental Research Department, Stoke Park Colony Bristol, and London School of Hygiene and Tropical Medicine

*CHRISTA B. ROSS, M.B., Ch.B., D.P.H., Deputy Medical Officer of Health, West Lothian

A. F. SKINNER, M.A., B.Sc., Ph.D., F.E.I.S., Professor of Education, University of St. Andrews

* Succeeded J. Miller Young 25th June 1948

v

N. T. WALKER, O.B.E., M.A., Ed.B., Ph.D., F.E.I.S., University of Aberdeen

†J. MILLER YOUNG, M.C., M.B., F.R.F.P. & S. (G.), D.P.H., Chief Executive School Medical Officer, Education Health Services, Glasgow

Ex officiis

R. R. RUSK, M.A., B.A., Ph.D., Director to the Scottish Council for Research in Education

A. J. BELFORD, J.P., M.A., F.E.I.S., Honorary Secretary to the Scottish Council for Research in Education

† Died 20th November 1947

PREFACE

THE inquiry reported in this volume was begun in the hope that it might throw light on the causes of a remarkable quantitative social fact, namely, that the results of intelligence tests show that the average score of members of large families is less than that of members of small families. It was feared that this might be leading to a steady fall in the national intelligence, if its cause is that intelligent parents are limiting their families. If, on the other hand, its cause is environmental, it is a duty to discover this and to strengthen the hand of social reformers. In either case the phenomenon is important, and to show beyond doubt that it really exists would be in itself worth while.

This at least our inquiry has done. The tables and diagrams of Chapter VII will, I think, convince any reader that the negative association between size of family and average intelligence score, whatever its cause, is undeniable. The only children averaged 42·0 points on the group test, those in families of two, 41·7 points, those in families of three, four and so on, averaged 38·3, 35·3, 32·5, 30·9, 29·5, 28·8, and in families of size nine, 27·97. The individuals in still larger families scored less again, on the average.

It should be unnecessary to say that this general tendency is quite compatible with the existence of very many exceptions. Many members of large families are, of course, highly intelligent. Whole families, with numerous members, are conspicuously clever. It is easy to bring forward such instances. But they do not disprove

the general trend shown in our tables and diagrams.
Moreover, this trend is found in diverse occupations and
classes. Thus among coalminers, large families are on
the average less able to attain high marks in tests;[1] and
in a group of advanced students in a London University
college the same tendency has been found.[2]

It should be equally unnecessary to say that the confir-
mation of the fact does not indicate in which direction the
causal connection works. The proof that large families
tend to be less intelligent[3] does not in itself indicate
whether they are large because they are unintelligent, or
unintelligent because they are large. It was hoped that
our inquiry might strengthen the one or the other hypothesis, although it was recognised that the intervention
of a war between 1932 and 1947 was a disturbing factor,
and, on the other hand, that increasing familiarity with
tests might have produced in the fifteen years a rise in
test performance: increasing familiarity not only, or indeed not chiefly, with tests themselves but with procedures in class teaching, in school reading books, in
newspaper " puzzle corners ", and in wireless broadcasts,
similar to those used in tests.

In the result we have found, in 1947 as compared with
1932, not only no fall in the average score, on the self-
same test, of a Scottish year group of eleven-year-olds
but an increase—quite a substantial increase from about
34·5 to about 36·7 points in a test with a maximum of
76 points. Undoubtedly this strengthens the environmental side of the argument—unless the increase is due
to that " test sophistication " spoken of in the previous
paragraph; unless, that is, the environmental influence

[1] H. E. G. Sutherland, *Journal of Educational Psychology*, 1929, XX,
pp. 81-90.

[2] H. Himmelweit, *Eugenics Review*, July 1948, XL, pp. 77-84.

[3] To avoid constant circumlocution I shall crave permission frequently to say simply " less, or more, intelligent ", when what I really
mean is " less, or more, able to attain high marks in a test ".

enables the children to answer the test more satisfactorily without raising their general intelligence. In the present volume we cannot prove or disprove this possibility, if indeed we ever can. But we hope to investigate it in time.

There are other possible explanations of the rise in average score, one of which is that it is due to a change in the distribution of family size between 1932 and 1947. If, as one interested correspondent puts it, the small families are nowadays not quite so small, and the large families not quite so large, this would explain a rise even on grounds of heredity. For it might mean that intelligent parents, although still restricting their families, are not doing this so much as formerly, and that less intelligent parents, on the other hand, are now to some extent restricting their families, so that the ratio of intelligent children to the population is now higher than formerly. Unfortunately, we do not know the distribution of family size in the 1932 survey, but inquiries are being made to see if we can supply this deficiency from other data.

Another hypothesis consistent with a differential birthrate and yet no fall in IQ (consistent, indeed, even with a rise as the general birthrate sinks) is that later-born children in a family tend to be less bright. This is referred to in Chapter VII, where data are given which go some way towards making this unlikely. As is there said, previous evidence is conflicting. It has indeed been claimed that later-born children are *more* intelligent, by L. L. Thurstone and Richard L. Jenkins,[1] but their

[1] *Order of Birth, Parent, Age and Intelligence,* University of Chicago Press, 1931. Their own sample of children were of low intelligence as a group. But they give details of a similar research by Miss M. Steckel, who drew a large sample of 6,790 children from 2,712 families and found a steady rise in IQ with birth order, the eighth-born being ·87 of a standard deviation superior to the first-born. There was apparently no relation between the ages of the parents, at the time of the child's birth, and its intelligence, except a tendency for children of parents of approximately the same age to be superior.

results have been disputed and their methods criticised. The reason why our present data are inconclusive on the relationship between intelligence and position in family is that, since all our children were aged eleven, those of them who are in an early position may be members of unfinished families which may increase, whereas the later-born, and especially the last-born (being now eleven) probably belong to finished families. There is thus a certain differential selection of parents when an age group of children is studied, and, moreover, the parents are of very varied ages.

We hope to make a direct attack on the influence of position by testing individually the siblings of our six-day sample as they grow up into the eleven-year-old group, using the same Terman-Merrill test, and, by thus testing always at eleven, avoiding any effect of possible blemishes in the age-standardisation of that test.

It is, of course, possible to construct hypothetical genetic theories of the inheritance of intelligence which would explain the co-existence of (i) a differential birth-rate (i.e. a negative association between family size and intelligence), and (ii) a permanent level of average intelligence, showing no decline. Those who have put forward hypotheses of this nature have been impressed by the possibility that a differential birthrate may have existed for centuries, and yet no noticeable fall in intelligence seems to have occurred. One such theory has been given by Professor Lionel Penrose in the *American Journal of Mental Deficiency* for July 1948. His illustrative model of a community in intellectual equilibrium is composed of a numerous superior class with a low birthrate, a less numerous inferior class with a high birthrate (about twice the former), and a small class of weaklings who do not survive, or at any rate are unable to have children. The superior class are all genetically AA, where A is the gene producing high intelligence. The inferior class are all Aa, that is, every one of them is a *carrier* of superior intelligence, although not personally showing it, since its expression is diluted by the other gene *a*. (A is not supposed to be either dominant or recessive.) Matings in the superior class produce only superiors (AA). Matings in the inferior class produce superior, inferior, and weaklings in the proportions 1: 2: 1. The weaklings cannot mate or produce offspring.

Such a community, with the classes in the proper proportion at outset, could remain in equilibrium despite the differential birthrate. But note that it is a peculiar differential birthrate—those of the lowest intelligence have no children at all. This is what keeps the average intelligence up in Penrose's artificial community. The hasty reader might imagine, especially from his last sentence before his summary,[1] that it is the high birthrate of the inferior class which does this, that the high birthrate of this class somehow prevents a fall in intelligence. On the contrary, it prevents a rise, which would occur if the inferior birthrate were less than twice that of the superior. It is necessary to keep up the size of the total population, if that is desired, but in doing so it replenishes the *a* genes, not the A, of which there is no loss except in the sense that the total population may be falling. These points are made quite clear by Professor Penrose if his paper is carefully read.

Such a compensatory mechanism as that advanced by Penrose may quite conceivably be the explanation of our results; for it to be in actual existence to-day it is not necessary that a class of very low IQs exist who have no children. Such do exist, but whether in sufficient numbers is doubtful. It would, however, be enough if very bad combinations (like *aa* in the crude simplification)

[1] It is: " For replacement of intelligence genes, lost on account of the relatively low fertility of the highly intelligent, the large birthrate of the supposedly inferior group is a necessity."

were not viable at all, but gave rise to unrecorded miscarriages.

All this, however, while interesting and a warning to us to be careful in drawing conclusions, is obviously highly speculative, even more so than the speculation that a genetic loss is actually going on and is merely being masked by environmental causes which can only be temporary and must be defeated in the long run by persistent selection. We cannot tell. We can only endeavour to accumulate evidence tending one way or the other, and meanwhile suspend judgment. " We are still in the field of speculation, where the only unforgivable mistake is to be certain."[1]

It must not be imagined that, as one friendly critic has put it, " you hoped for a fall in average score, and now that you have instead found a rise, you are trying to explain it away ". Of course we did not hope for a fall. We feared there might be one. Our fears have happily not been realised. But, to reverse Clough's well-known line, we must remember that " if fears were liars, hopes may be dupes ": we must see to it that we are not deceived in our strengthened hope that national intelligence is not falling: we must examine (and, let us hope, find that we can refute) every conceivable explanation which may leave open the possibility that adverse selection is still going on behind a façade of temporary improvement. And our rich accumulation of data may enable us to do at least some of this in time.

In addition to our group-test results from well over 70,000 children, we have Binet-test results from over 1000 of them, as we had in 1932. They confirm the negative association of intelligence with family size. Unfortunately, however, the comparison of 1947 with 1932 is not so direct. The sample tested individually in 1932,

[1] Magnus Wechsler writing (on quite another matter) in " The Times " of 1st January 1949.

although pretty good, was not quite as representative as the sample in 1947: and in 1932 the Stanford, in 1947 the Terman-Merrill, Revisions of the Binet test were used, forms which are not identical and likewise differ in standardisation.[1] Careful statistical refinements have been used in Chapter VIII to extract as much information as possible from these imperfect data, and the verdict of that chapter is that no change in average IQ can be deduced from them. That does not prove that there has been no change, but it denies that any change is proven, in either direction. We all, however, including the writer of that chapter, recognise that the above-noted difficulties, and especially the small number of children examined by both forms of the test, make its conclusions insecure. We are continuing the work of comparing the two versions of the Terman Revisions more adequately.

If, as we hope, our survey is again repeated by our successors in fifteen or twenty years' time, they will do well to note the recommendation made in Chapter VIII, that it is more important to use exactly the same individual test, rather than the same group test, provided the latter correlates highly with the former. But they may decide on quite another form of survey, taking whole families instead of an age group. Better still, they may do both.

Another finding of the group test is that girls have improved in average score more than boys. This is only

[1] Even although these difficulties make the 1947 Terman-Merrill test less useful, or at any rate less immediately useful, as a help in comparing the present with the past, we must remember that the magnificent work of those who carried out the 1947 individual testing has a value in itself. To have a very representative sample (the six-day sample) of a complete year group of a country tested by efficient and trained testers gives us in the first place an admirable estimate of Scotland's intelligence in comparison with the western United States, where this test was standardised and in the second place must be of value to those who did that standardisation, as an application of their work likely to show up any weaknesses. For example, we suspect that the Terman-Merrill test favours boys.

in accordance with what we have been finding with Moray House tests for the past six or eight years, though the difference now appears to be fading away again. On tests in which boys and girls formerly did equally well, girls began during the war years to draw ahead of boys. This may possibly be due to the war, which perhaps disturbed boys in their devotion to studies more than it did girls. Or perhaps the girls, during black-out years, stayed at home more than boys, and read more. The difference cannot easily be explained by any selective process, and would appear to be environmental. Perhaps girls, more docile and obedient than boys (I am told!) have acquired more " test-sophistication ".

And then, most curiously, the verdict is reversed on the Terman-Merrill test, where the boys do better than the girls. One reaction to all this may be, indeed has been in the case of one of our number, a disparagement of all intelligence tests, or at least of group intelligence tests, except when used for average results only and not in individual cases. This, I myself feel, would be unfortunate, and I believe it to be untrue. I have had for thirty years a very wide experience of making, using, and following up the results of group tests. Few can be more fully aware of their dangers and pitfalls than I am. They are, of course, like all human instruments, far from infallible: but they are less fallible than most other methods of estimating human ability—at any rate, at estimating ability in a comparatively short time, as is often necessary. We must not make the better the enemy of the good. It is a common error of judgment to say (as one can of most things) " this is not perfect ", and then to add " so away with it ". Of course group intelligence tests are not perfect. But in the absence of any better alternative at present, we must use the group tests and their correlations with the numerous social facts we have collected, while bearing in mind throughout the very

many limitations to which these tests are subject. At
the same time, our ability to interpret the group-test
results is greatly increased by the existence of individual-
test data for a sample of the age group.

The analysis of the sociological data for the whole
group, and the still richer data for the thirty-six-day sample, is going on, as is also a study of the five hundred odd
pairs of twins. Future volumes adumbrated in Chapter
IX will describe the results. The Mental Survey Committee wishes also to embark on a long-term project,
nothing less than a " follow-up " (lasting twenty years
or more) of 2000 of the children tested in this survey;
and it is not without hope that financial support may be
forthcoming to make this possible. The 2000 in question
would be composed of the six-day sample, for whom we
have an individual Terman-Merrill intelligence quotient,
plus about 400 of the most intelligent, and 400 of the
least intelligent, of the others. The six-day sample forms
a complete cross-section of Scottish children, drawn proportionately from all grades of intelligence, and will be
invaluable in many ways. The addition of the two ex-
treme groups increases the numbers at those parts of the
distribution where frequency is low, and will enable the
future careers of these two very important classes to be
studied adequately. If we can obtain the necessary co-
operation and support to do this, the 2000 children whose
careers we shall follow can be assured of sympathy and
of complete anonymity. No names will ever be betrayed.
The group will be a cross-section of the children born in
Scotland in 1936, ranging over the whole scale of intelligence, born in every month of the year, from different
social classes, from Lowlands, Highlands and Islands,
from village, city and town, from large families and from
small. And not only the 2000 themselves, but their
brothers and sisters. A Scotland in miniature. Our hope
is that from this work we, or rather our successors, may

learn how to smooth the path of the able, to help along the less well endowed, to give guidance about schooling and careers, to advise those in authority who make regulations and control finance, and generally to help Scotland and Scots yet unborn to a life of greater happiness, of less hardship, and less frustration.

In an investigation as extensive as ours of 1947, the helpers were too numerous to mention individually in a preface. A list has accordingly been appended. The whole research was an extraordinary example of team work (entirely unpaid); for all directors of education and their staffs, teachers in all schools, all medical officers of health, all district nurses, students and lecturers in the training colleges, many retired teachers, several university professors, and still others had a share in the project, and, of course, the children and their parents too deserve our warm thanks, as also do the Scottish Education Department and the Local Education Authorities. The Committee must make special reference to its secretary, Miss Ann Kennedy, without whose methodical care, unfailing courtesy, and unflagging industry we should indeed have been overwhelmed by the magnitude of the job. And finally they make grateful acknowledgment to the Nuffield Foundation and the Eugenics Society for the grants which financed the research, and to the Scottish Council for Research in Education for bearing the cost of publication of this volume.

GODFREY THOMSON,
Chairman.

CONTENTS

ACKNOWLEDGMENTS

The Scottish Education Department, the Educational Institute of Scotland, and Education Committees for permission to undertake the survey.

Administration

D. M. McIntosh, M.A., B.Sc., B.Ed., Ph.D., F.R.S.E., F.E.I.S.
Directors of Education
Head Teachers and Teachers of Authority Schools, of Private and Independent Schools, of Schools for Problem and Handicapped Children, and of Residential and Certified Institutions and Approved Schools

Sociological Inquiry

J. G. Kyd, C.B.E., Registrar-General
*J. Miller Young, M.C., M.B., F.R.F.P. & S.(G), D.P.H.
†A. Anderson, M.A., M.D., D.P.H., D.P.A.
Medical Officers of Health of Counties and Burghs and School Medical Officers. The Queen's Institute of District Nursing, Scottish Branch. Health Visitors, School Nurses and District Nurses

Individual Testing

D. Kennedy-Fraser, M.A., B.Sc., F.R.S.E.
Norman T. Walker, O.B.E., M.A., Ed.B., Ph.D., F.E.I.S. (Aberdeen)
Margaret Young, M.A., B.Ed. (Dundee)
Edith I. M. Thomson, M.A., B.Ed. (Edinburgh)
Organisers and testers in other areas, including Directors of Education, Education Committee Psychologists, Head Teachers and Students

* Died 20th November 1947
† Died 22nd December 1948

Correction of Scripts

A. J. Belford, J.P., M.A., F.E.I.S.

J. Maxwell, M.A., B.Ed.

The Directors of Studies of Aberdeen, Dundee, Moray House and Jordanhill Training Colleges; the Principals of Craiglockhart R.C. and Notre Dame R.C. Training Colleges

Directors of Education of Ayrshire, Clackmannan, East Lothian, Fife, Kirkcudbright, and Perth and Kinross

Local Branches of the Educational Institute in Dundee, Glasgow, Bute, Clackmannan, Dumfriesshire, Orkney, Renfrewshire and Zetland

Ex-Teachers of the Edinburgh Branch of the Educational Institute

Students of Aberdeen, Dundee, Moray House, Jordanhill, Craiglockhart R.C. and Notre Dame R.C. Training Colleges

Coding Sociological Schedules

J. Maxwell, M.A., B.Ed.

D. V. Glass, B.Sc. (Econ)., Ph.D.

Students of Moray House Training College

Sorting Data

J. Maxwell, M.A., B.Ed.

Calculations

A. C. Aitken, F.R.S., F.R.S.E., M.A., D.Sc.

D. N. Lawley, M.A., D.Sc.

J. Maxwell, M.A., B.Ed.

D. A. Walker, M.A., B.Ed., Ph.D., F.R.S.E.

LIST OF TABLES

LIST OF FIGURES

ANALYSIS OF CONTENTS

I

INTRODUCTION

PREVIOUS SURVEYS

THE most ambitious project which the Research Council ventured to undertake in the early years of its existence was the 1932 Mental Survey involving the testing by a group intelligence test of a complete age group of Scottish school children numbering almost ninety thousand.[1] As the group test only admitted of the mean and standard deviation being computed, to determine the IQ of the age group a thousand of the pupils whose scores in the group test were known, referred to usually as " The Binet Thousand ", were tested individually by the 1916 Stanford Revision of the Binet scale. These pupils proved to be a slightly superior sample, and to correct this defect and supplement the 1932 group survey the Research Council decided on another survey of such an unbiased sample as could be individually tested by one tester within a reasonable time. To satisfy this requirement it was decided to apply the 1916 Stanford Revision with very slight modifications to suit Scottish conditions, to all children in Scotland born on 1st February, 1st May, 1st August and 1st November in the year 1926. This sample numbered 874, of whom 444 were boys and 430 girls. The results gave a mean IQ for the group of 100·11 and a standard deviation of 15·58. The investigation is

[1] An account of this survey is published in *The Intelligence of Scottish Children*. Publications of the Scottish Council for Research in Education, V. London: University of London Press, Ltd., 1933.

reported in *The Intelligence of a Representative Group of Scottish Children.*[1]

INTENTION TO REPEAT 1932 SURVEY

At the time of the original survey the Research Council had in mind the desirability of repeating the 1932 survey on some future occasion, and had made its dispositions for such a repetition. The material that could conveniently be preserved was stored, and indications attached giving instructions and advice for any later application. Whereas no definite interval was contemplated, it was nevertheless felt that only after a lapse of twenty-five years would such a repetition be profitable.

ORIGIN OF 1947 SURVEY

At the Annual Meeting in June 1945 Professor Godfrey Thomson brought to the attention of the Research Council a suggestion made by Dr J. A. Fraser Roberts and conveyed to Professor Thomson by Sir Alexander Carr-Saunders, Chairman of the Population Investigation Committee, that in view of the presumed decline of national intelligence by reason of the differential birth-rate[2] the Research Council should undertake a repetition of the 1932 mental survey, applying the same test to the corresponding age group, to secure evidence as to whether there had been any change since the original application.

The request of the Population Investigation Committee raised several issues:

(1) whether the time was opportune for another survey; this resolved itself into

(*a*) whether a sufficient interval had elapsed to make a difference discernible;

[1] A. M. Macmeeken. Publications of the Scottish Council for Research in Education, XV. London: University of London Press, Ltd., 1939.

[2] See e.g., *The Trend of National Intelligence* by Godfrey Thomson. Occasional Papers on Eugenics, Number Three. London: The Eugenics Society and Hamish Hamilton Medical Books, 1947.

(*b*) whether the conditions in the schools made it desirable to hold a survey;

(2) which of the two previous surveys should be repeated—the group survey of 1932 or the individual survey of 1937;

(3) whether in the circumstances a survey was administratively practicable;

(4) by whom was the cost of the survey to be defrayed.

After preliminary discussion by the Executive Committee of the Research Council a conference was held in Edinburgh on 16th March 1946 at which the Population Investigation Committee was represented by

Sir Alexander Carr-Saunders
Dr J. A. Fraser Roberts
Professor D. V. Glass

and the Research Council by members of the Executive Committee and the Director.

At this conference the argument advanced by the Population Investigation Committee was that, although many attempts had been made to ascertain inferentially whether the average intelligence of the community was declining, the only way to clinch the issue was to measure at one point in time and to repeat the measurement at another point in time; the Research Council 1932 mental survey afforded an admirable instrument for this purpose; in no other place was it possible to repeat such a measurement on such a scale.

Doubt was nevertheless expressed by representatives of the Research Council as to the expediency of the repetition. The first objection was that the proposed repetition was too close to the original testing, but they were assured that, although the interpretation of the results might be rendered more difficult by the shortness of the interval, no objection could be sustained against the statistical reliability of the survey on that ground. An assumption made by the usual group intelligence tests is that the children tested have had a reasonable exposure to educational influences during their lifetime, whereas children tested in 1947 would have had six years of war in their lives, four of these at school; school work had been dislocated by war conditions; and many of the children were suffering from emotional disturbances originated during evacuation. To counterbalance these handicaps it was recalled that the 1932 group might have been adversely affected by the years of depression between 1926 and 1932.

The difference in the size of the sample inclined the statisticians to press for the group rather than for an individual survey, as by reason of the greater numbers participating in the group testing even a small difference would be significant.

While too much stress, it was conceded, should not be laid on the administrative difficulties of such an investigation, it was admittedly asking much of educational officials fully occupied with the salvaging of the wreckage left by the war years and at the same time engaged in bringing into force the provisions of the 1946 Education (Scotland) Act, to impose on themselves the additional burden of the survey. When the social significance of the results was indicated to them, the directors of education nevertheless most considerately consented to co-operate. An assurance was also given by the Educational Institute of Scotland that, provided the teachers were not required to undertake the correction of the scripts, the survey would have their support.

The Population Investigation Committee agreed to relieve the Research Council of the whole expense of the survey, which, apart from publication of the report, was to cost about £4000. This cost has been met out of a grant made to the Population Investigation Committee by the Nuffield Foundation, and by an additional grant of £2000 given to the Committee for this purpose by the Eugenics Society. Thanks are due to both these bodies for their generous help, without which the inquiry could not have been undertaken.

EXTENSION OF SURVEY

Encouraged by the support it received from these quarters, the Research Council not only consented to sponsor the survey, but recognising that a mere repetition of the 1932 survey would not contribute anything of immediate value to educational research, decided that the opportunity should be seized of enlarging its scope to that of a true sociological inquiry which might not only be directed to investigating the issue with which the Population Investigation Committee was concerned, but might also provide additional data of value to the Council.

PRELIMINARY ARRANGEMENTS

Immediately the proposal to conduct another survey was mooted, although no decision had as yet been taken as to the form the survey would take or what test should be applied, the 1932 test was as a precautionary measure withdrawn from the market.

A guess as to the numbers likely to comprise the eleven-year-old group in 1947 was hazarded, the figure named being 80,000. The estimate supplied later by the Registrar-General gave the number of children aged 11 at mid-June 1947 as males 40,800, females 39,500, total 80,300,[1] and the number who actually took the test was 70,805, compared with the Registrar-General's estimate of 100,300 and the 87,498 taking the test in the 1932 survey.

[1] Scotland's population at 30th June 1947 was 5,138,700, according to statement made by the Secretary of State for Scotland in the House of Commons (*Glasgow Herald*, 6th August 1947).

C

APPOINTMENT OF MENTAL SURVEY COMMITTEE

At a meeting held on 31st May 1946 the Executive Committee of the Research Council proceeded to the appointment of a committee to deal with the projected mental survey. It was agreed to invite the following to join the committee:

Professor Godfrey Thomson

Mr D. Kennedy-Fraser

Dr D. M. McIntosh (representative of Directors of Education on the Research Council)

Mr W. L. McKinlay and Mr A. M. Orr (representatives of the Educational Institute on the Research Council)

Professor A. F. Skinner and Dr N. T. Walker (representatives of Universities and Training Colleges on the Research Council)

A School Medical Officer to be nominated by the Association of School Medical Officers of Scotland

Dr J. A. Fraser Roberts

Professor D. V. Glass

Professor Thomson was named chairman. The committee was given power to co-opt.

The committee as finally constituted appears on pp. v-vi.

II
ADMINISTRATIVE ARRANGEMENTS
COMPARISON WITH 1932 SURVEY

THE administration of the 1947 mental survey was in certain respects easier than that of the survey of 1932, but in others more difficult. It was easier in so far as those responsible for the earlier experiment left full details of an organisation which had been a proved success. It was more difficult because of the conditions in the schools and the extended scope of the inquiry.

Even in ordinary circumstances such a survey would be no mean undertaking, but the 1947 survey fell at a time when conditions were far from being ordinary. The schools had not fully recovered from war conditions —evacuation, destruction of, or damage to, buildings, and shortage of teachers. In addition to these difficulties the administrative staffs were faced with the problems arising out of the raising of the school leaving age.

The extent of the 1947 survey was very much greater than that carried out in 1932. As stated earlier, it was necessary to make much more comprehensive the information which the survey sought to elicit regarding the pupils. The Mental Survey Committee felt, however, that it was an impossible task to obtain the full sociological information for all pupils, and decided to collect these data for a random sample only; the minimum information was asked for all pupils. It can be readily understood how the administration became somewhat complex in its efforts to define clearly the pupils for whom the different data were required.

7

The successful administration of the survey required the permission of the Scottish Education Department to authorise the dislocation of the school work necessitated by taking from their classes on the day of the test the pupils of the age group to be tested; of the education authorities who are the managers of the schools, and of the governors of the private schools. Equally essential was the co-operation and goodwill of the directors of education to organise the distribution and collection of the tests and forms; of the school staffs to apply the tests and secure the sociological data for all pupils; and of the medical officers of health to obtain the fuller sociological information for the random sample.

PERMISSION GRANTED

Scottish Education Department and Education Authorities

No difficulty was experienced in obtaining the permission of the Scottish Education Department and the education authorities. The Secretary of the Department said in his reply:

I am directed to refer to your letter of 9th May intimating the decision of the Council, on the request of the Population Investigation Committee, to conduct in the first week of June, 1947, a group mental survey of pupils of the 11-year age group in Scottish schools, and to say that the Department for their part have no objection to the proposal. They assume, however, that every effort will be made in carrying out the survey to avoid imposing any avoidable burdens on teachers and education authorities.

Directors of Education

The directors of education had agreed to support the Scottish Council for Research in Education in carrying out a repetition of the 1932 survey, but they expressed grave doubts about the necessity for the additional sociological inquiry. It was regarded as advisable, therefore, that a deputation from the Mental Survey Committee should meet the Association of Directors of Education to convince them of the urgency and the importance of the undertaking. Professor Thomson, Professor Glass and Dr Fraser Roberts met the Executive Committee of the Association of Directors of Education, and were able to report to the committee that the directors would give their whole-hearted support to the complete survey.

Private Schools

If Section 109 of the Education (Scotland) Act, 1946, requiring the Scottish Education Department to keep a register of independent schools had been in operation, no difficulty would have been occasioned in communicating with all the private schools in Scotland. The survey, however, anticipated the implementing of the Section, and inquiries had to be addressed to the directors of education asking for the names and addresses of the private schools known to them in their respective areas. While some of these schools took up the project enthusiastically, it was only after personal letters from the chairman of the Survey Committee had been addressed to the heads of other schools that they agreed to participate. The number of independent schools actually taking part was 91, with 1,844 pupils, compared with 99 schools and 1,629 pupils in the 1932 survey. The main reason given by the private schools refusing to co-operate was the difficulty in securing the data to answer the inquiries contained in the sociological schedules.

Special Schools and Institutions

The number of special schools and institutions has increased since the 1932 survey, but less difficulty was experienced in tracing them.

In these establishments testing was undertaken only when the pupil's handicap would not invalidate the test. Care was taken to ascertain how many pupils with such a handicap were included in the age group.

PROCEDURE

The carrying out of the survey required the use of:

(1) a group intelligence test set to all pupils born in 1936 (see *The Intelligence of Scottish Children*, pp. 136-42);

(2) a short sociological schedule for all pupils born in 1936 (see Appendix I, p. 36).

(3) a more extensive random-sample sociological schedule for all pupils born on the 1st, 2nd and 3rd days of each month in 1936, and for all twins born in 1936 (see Appendix II, p. 38);

(4) individual tests (Terman-Merrill) for about 1,200 pupils to calibrate the group test (see Chapter IV).

GROUP INTELLIGENCE TEST

In order to reproduce the test situation of the 1932 survey exactly, the original form of the test and its preliminary practice sheet were used.

To avoid the effect of practice in the performance of tests, directors of education in areas where it was customary to apply intelligence tests for promotion purposes, were requested to postpone, if possible, the application of such tests to pupils born in 1936 until after the survey in June. As all directors could not accede to this request, it was decided that a question should be incorporated in the sociological schedule asking whether the pupil had been previously tested by a group test during the session 1946-7.

Great care was taken to ensure that it was not generally known that the 1932 mental survey test was to be used.

The test, including preliminary practice sheet, was set in all schools on Wednesday, 4th June 1947. One or two private schools had desired to apply the test on another date, but agreement to apply it on the proper date was secured.

Directors of education were given the choice of having

the scripts sent direct to the schools from the printers or sent in bulk to the education offices. The completed scripts were returned from the schools to the directors of education, who were asked to retain them until they were called in by the Research Council. The storage and correction of 80,000 tests were problems which could not easily be solved by the staff of the Research Council, and other assistance had to be sought. The marking and checking are dealt with in Chapter V.

In the case of the private schools the tests were sent from, and were returned direct to, the Research Council. Detailed instructions for the administration of the test were sent to each school.

SOCIOLOGICAL SCHEDULE

Sociological schedules for each pupil born in 1936 were sent to the directors of education early in May, along with instructions to head teachers. The completed schedules and the worked intelligence tests were returned in separate bundles to the directors.

RANDOM-SAMPLE SOCIOLOGICAL SCHEDULE

This schedule was completed for all pupils born on the 1st, 2nd and 3rd days of each month in 1936, and for all twins born in 1936. The names of these pupils were obtained on rolls issued to the schools in January.

For these pupils accordingly there were two schedules, (a) the SOCIOLOGICAL SCHEDULE, and (b) the RANDOM-SAMPLE SOCIOLOGICAL SCHEDULE. The first seventeen questions of the random-sample sociological schedule were identical with those on the sociological schedule. As soon as these seventeen questions were completed the random-sample sociological schedules were returned by the schools to the directors of education, who forwarded them to the Research Council. Full details regarding this schedule will be found in Chapter III.

INDIVIDUAL TESTING

A description of this part of the investigation is given in Chapter IV.

GROUP TESTING

The administration of a group test of intelligence to a complete age group accommodated in some 3000 schools was in itself no mean task, but the additional complication of the sociological schedules and the individual testing added a burden which might have resulted in such a breakdown of the arrangements that the results would have been of little value. Sufficient tribute can hardly be paid to the directors of education and the teaching staffs for the way in which they carried out the instructions issued by the Research Council. The group test was administered throughout the country practically without a hitch. Some difficulty was experienced with the sociological schedules and still more with the random-sample schedules; but it can safely be said that this did not in any way prejudice the results of the investigation.

CIRCULARS AND FORMS

A clearer idea of the administration of the survey may be formed from a study of the relevant circulars and forms. Only those to the local authority schools are given, but the circulars to the private schools differed merely in details.

(1) REQUEST FOR PERMISSION

(a) LETTER TO DIRECTORS OF EDUCATION

The Scottish Council for Research in Education, after considerable hesitation, has agreed to the request of the Population Investigation Committee to undertake a group mental survey similar to that conducted in 1932 in order to secure evidence for the Royal Commission on Population to determine whether or not there has been any decline in intelligence in the interval between the two surveys. To render the results more instructive it is proposed to utilise such information regarding the children tested as is contained on the national record card.

It is realised that at the present time authorities are under exceptional pressure, but it is hoped that by reason of the social and national significance of the findings they will see their way to agree to co-operate in this project. The minimum of work will be expected of teachers and directors of education, and as the majority of areas have had considerable experience in the administration of intelligence tests, it is anticipated that the testing of an age group will be a relatively easy matter. The test will require only about one hour of the pupil's time. Sufficient copies for the pupils in your area will be supplied free, and any costs incurred, for example, postages, will be defrayed by the Research Council.

For the purposes of the inquiry it is essential that the conditions under which the test is given will approximate as closely as possible to those of the previous survey. The complete 1936 age group will be tested during the first week in June.

I shall be glad if you will place this request before your committee at the earliest opportunity.

(b) LETTER TO HEAD TEACHERS OF SCHOOLS FOR PROBLEM AND HANDICAPPED CHILDREN

The Scottish Council for Research in Education, after considerable hesitation, has agreed to the request of the Population Investigation Committee to undertake in 1947 a group mental survey of eleven-year-old pupils similar to that conducted in 1932, in order to secure evidence for the Royal Commission on Population to determine whether or not there has been any decline in intelligence in the interval between the two surveys.

The directors of education of the various areas have agreed to undertake the administrative arrangements involved in the survey. As residential special schools are not included in the arrangements of the directors, and as by reason of the social and national significance of the survey it is highly desirable that the age group tested should be completely representative, the Research Council invites your co-operation in the project.

The Mental Survey Committee would be extremely obliged if you would indicate how many of your pupils are in a position to take a group test of intelligence and, for statistical purposes only, how many cannot do so—boys and girls separately. The survey will take place during the first week in June.

As full instructions for the administration of the test will be supplied, the testing will not involve the entrance to the school of any outsider. The scoring of the test will be undertaken by the Research Council, and the results of pupils and of individual schools will be kept strictly confidential.

The test will require only about one hour of the pupil's time. Sufficient copies will be supplied free, and any costs incurred, e.g. postages, will be defrayed by the Research Council.

To render the results more instructive, it is proposed to obtain additional information, if available, regarding the children, such as height, weight, and father's occupation.

A prepaid addressed envelope is enclosed for reply, which will be much appreciated.

(2) SOCIOLOGICAL SCHEDULES—
RANDOM-SAMPLE NOMINAL ROLL

(a) LETTER TO DIRECTORS OF EDUCATION

I enclose a copy of the sociological schedule which is to be completed for all pupils included in the survey. It will be clear that the questions have been reduced to a minimum and that, in the main, only such information regarding the pupils has been asked as is contained on the national record card.

In order to obtain fuller information, a more detailed sociological schedule will be employed for a representative sample of the pupils. Another sample of about one thousand pupils will be tested individually by the Terman-Merrill scale to calibrate the group test. It is proposed to draw these two samples from the children born on the first three days of each month of 1936.

As the individual testing must be undertaken as soon as possible, I should be glad if you would obtain the necessary information for me at your earliest convenience. I enclose a specimen letter to teachers, along with the forms on which the names and dates of birth of children should be entered. I should be glad if you would issue these to the schools in your area and let me have them, if possible, before 15th February. It is important that *nil* returns should be made.

(b). Specimen Letter to Head Teachers
(To be adapted to local needs)

As you are doubtless aware, the Scottish Council for Research in Education has decided to undertake a mental survey similar to that conducted in 1932. This project has received the approval of the Scottish Education Department, the Educational Institute of Scotland and the education committee of your area. The Research Council is relying on your co-operation and the co-operation of your staff.

The object of the survey is to secure evidence for the Population Investigation Committee to determine whether or not there has been any decline in intelligence in the interval between the two surveys, and it is only the social and national significance of the findings that has induced the Research Council to undertake the survey.

In order to obtain fuller information, a more detailed sociological schedule will be employed for a representative sample of the pupils. Another sample of about one thousand pupils will be tested individually by the Terman-Merrill scale to calibrate the group test. It is proposed to draw these two samples from the children born on the first three days of each month of 1936.

I should be obliged if you would complete the attached form and return it to the director of education at your earliest convenience. If there are no children in your school born on the above dates, please make a *nil* return.

ROLL of (*a*) all Pupils born on 1st, 2nd and 3rd of each month in 1936;
(*b*) all Twins, other than those born on 1st, 2nd and 3rd of
each month, born in 1936.

Name of County or City/County...

Name of school.. Official Number of school............

Postal address...

Number of pupils on roll in last session........ Number of full-time teachers........

Give names in the following order:

Boys born on 1st, 2nd and 3rd of each month in 1936;

Girls born on 1st, 2nd and 3rd of each month in 1936;

Twins born in 1936, other than those born on 1st, 2nd and 3rd of each
month.

If child has a twin, indicate with a T.

NAMES Surname first, to be entered in order of birth Jan. 1st, 2nd, 3rd, Feb. 1st, 2nd, 3rd, etc.	Date of Birth		Sex B or G	Twins T	For Office Use only
	Day	Month			
1.........					
2.........					
3.........					
4.........					
5.........					
6.........					
7.........					
8.........					
9.........					
10.........					
11.........					
12.........					
13.........					
14.........					
15.........					
16.........					
17.........					
18.........					
19.........					
20.........					
21.........					
22.........					
23.........					
24.........					
25.........					

NOTE.—Enter the word " Nil " if there are no children in your school born
on the dates concerned.

TO BE COMPLETED AND RETURNED AS SOON AS POSSIBLE

(3) GROUP TEST—ADMINISTRATIVE ARRANGEMENTS

(a) LETTER TO DIRECTORS OF EDUCATION

In order to plan the arrangements for the administration of the intelligence test to the complete 1936 age group, the information asked for on the enclosed form is required. I shall be obliged if you will complete and return it to me at your earliest convenience.

I. *Intelligence Test*

The test is to be set to all pupils in the 1936 age group during the first week in June. A preliminary practice test, lasting for ten minutes, will be set to the pupils just prior to the test proper. Wherever possible, the test should be set on *Wednesday, 4th June*. If this is impossible, directors are asked to indicate the day on which it will be convenient to set the test.

II. *Administration of the Test*

Directors may choose to have the tests sent (a) in bulk for distribution to the schools, or (b) direct from the printer to the schools.

III. *Use of Objective Tests in the Area*

There has been a considerable increase in the use of standardised tests of intelligence and attainment. This may have some effect on the results of the tests, and so some indication is needed of the extent to which tests have been introduced since 1932.

IV. *Return of the Scripts*

An assurance has been given that no cost for the administration of the survey will fall on the local authority. Directors may choose either to submit an account of the total cost or to allow each head teacher to send direct a note of the postages incurred.

(*b*) FORM SENT TO DIRECTORS OF EDUCATION

To be completed at your earliest convenience and returned to
Dr Douglas M. McIntosh, 46 Moray Place, Edinburgh, 3

1. Education area ....

2. Date selected for the test...

3. If tests are to be sent in bulk for distribution from Education
   Offices:

   (*a*) Number of schools in which pupils are to be tested............
   (*b*) Total number of pupils to be tested............

4. If tests are to be sent direct from printer to schools, please return
   with this form a list of schools showing:

   (*a*) Postal address
   (*b*) Nearest railway station
   (*c*) Number of pupils to be tested in each school

5. *Use of Objective Tests in Area*

   Are pupils in your area tested with a group intelligence test
   and/or standardised achievement tests?   YES/NO
   If yes,

   (*a*) Which tests are used? ....
   ....
   ....
   ....

   (*b*) Age at which children are tested..

   Signature...
                              Director of Education

   Date...

(4) OUTLINE OF INVESTIGATION

LETTER TO DIRECTORS OF EDUCATION

In order to acquaint directors of education with the administrative arrangements for the survey the following outline may prove helpful. If you have any comments to make on these, I should be glad if you would let me have them immediately. The investigation involves:

(1) a group intelligence test set to all pupils born in 1936;
(2) a short sociological schedule for all pupils born in 1936;

(3) a more extensive random-sample sociological schedule for all pupils born on the 1st, 2nd and 3rd days of each month in 1936, and for all twins born in 1936;
(4) individual testing (Terman-Merrill) of about one thousand pupils to calibrate the group test.

1. Group Intelligence Test

The test will be set on Wednesday, 4th June, to all pupils born in 1936. The scripts will be sent either directly to the schools or in bulk to the director of education. All scripts should be returned from the schools to the director, who should retain them until they are called in by the Research Council. It will be understood that the Council does not have facilities to cope with the correction of the 80,000 tests at one time.

The correction of the tests will be undertaken by the Council, unless any director wishes to undertake the correction of the tests in his own area.

The number of tests for each area has been asked for by the circular letter dated 19th March.

2. Sociological Schedule

The sociological schedule to be completed by the teachers for all children born in 1936 is in the form agreed upon by the Association of Directors of Education.

The schedules will be forwarded to the directors, along with instructions to head teachers, as soon as they have been printed. The completed schedules should be returned by the schools to the director of education, along with the worked intelligence tests. Head teachers will be asked to parcel the schedules and tests together, each in a separate bundle securely tied.

3. Random-Sample Sociological Schedule

The random sample consists of all children born on the 1st, 2nd and 3rd days of each month in 1936, and all twins born in 1936. The names of these children were obtained on the rolls issued with the circular letter dated 24th January 1947.

For the children in the random sample there will be two schedules: (1) the SOCIOLOGICAL SCHEDULE, and (2) the RANDOM-SAMPLE SOCIOLOGICAL SCHEDULE. The first seventeen questions of the random-sample sociological schedule are identical with those on the sociological schedule. These will be completed by the teacher and the remainder by investigators appointed by the Council.

Random-sample schedules, along with the rolls, will be sent to directors of education for distribution to the appropriate schools. As soon as the first seventeen questions have been completed, the schedules will be returned to the director of education, who will forward them to the Research Council, so that the remainder of the schedule may be completed.

N.B.—*Only the Random-Sample Schedule will be returned immediately*

4. Individual Testing

This will be done by qualified testers. It is hoped that the director of education will afford facilities for the test to be administered to any selected pupil who happens to be attending a school in his area.

(5) SOCIOLOGICAL SCHEDULES

(a) LETTER TO DIRECTORS OF EDUCATION

The following items are being forwarded to you this week:

1. ....copies of the sociological schedule.
2. ....copies of the random-sample sociological schedule.
3. ....rolls of pupils in random sample.
4. ....copies of letter to head teachers (general instructions).

I should be obliged if you would forward these at your earliest convenience to the schools in your area. I also enclose a draft circular to schools, which you can adapt to suit your own circumstances.

The random-sample sociological schedules should be returned to you from the schools, along with the rolls, immediately the first seventeen questions have been completed. The other questions of these schedules are to be dealt with by investigators appointed by the Research Council; early return of these schedules to the Research Council will be appreciated.

The completed sociological schedules should be retained by the schools until the pupils have taken the intelligence test. The completed schedules, along with the worked tests, should be retained in your office until called in by the Research Council.

There may be alterations in the number of pupils in the random sample or in the age group since the original returns were made. Additional copies of both schedules have been included to meet this contingency.

(b) SPECIMEN LETTER FROM DIRECTORS OF EDUCATION TO HEAD TEACHERS
Sociological Schedules

1. {I enclose
{I have to-day forwarded to you under separate cover

   (1) ....copies of the sociological schedule.

   (2) ....copies of the random-sample sociological schedule.

   (3) The roll of pupils in your school in the random sample.

   (4) Letter to head teachers (general instructions).

2. Random-Sample Sociological Schedule

Kindly complete the first seventeen questions of this schedule at your earliest convenience and return the schedules to me, along with the roll of pupils.

If there are no pupils in your school in the random sample, kindly return the roll immediately.

There may be alterations in your roll of pupils in the random sample. If a pupil has left, enter a note on the roll to this effect; if an additional pupil has been enrolled in your school, enter his or her name and send for an additional random-sample sociological schedule.

3. Sociological Schedule

The questions on this schedule are identical with the first seventeen questions of the random-sample schedule. Complete these questions and retain these schedules until the pupils have taken the intelligence test.

On Wednesday, 4th June, after the intelligence test has been administered, head teachers should parcel the completed schedules and worked tests, each in a separate bundle securely tied, and forward them together to me.

Kindly inform me if additional schedules are required.

D

(6) GROUP INTELLIGENCE TEST—ISSUE OF TESTS

(*a*) LETTER TO DIRECTORS OF EDUCATION

I have to inform you that the intelligence tests and instructions have been forwarded to you.
your schools.

Additional tests have also been forwarded to you to cover any increase in the number of pupils in any school.

I should be glad if you would acknowledge receipt of the tests to the Research Council on the enclosed postcard.

Enclosed is a specimen circular to head teachers informing them that the tests have been dispatched from the printer or by you. It would be helpful if you would ensure that every school in your area acknowledges receipt of the tests.

(*b*) SPECIMEN LETTER FROM DIRECTORS OF EDUCATION TO HEAD TEACHERS

I have to inform you that the intelligence tests and instructions have been forwarded to you (to-day). Kindly acknowledge receipt of the tests and instructions to me *immediately* they are received.

If there is an increase in the number of pupils to be tested, please apply to me for additional tests.

Kindly forward to me the completed tests, along with the sociological schedules, on the day after the date of the test.

(*c*) TO HEAD TEACHERS OF AUTHORITY SCHOOLS

In a previous communication intimation was given of the Mental Survey to be conducted by the Research Council in June of this year. The investigation involves:

(1) setting a group intelligence test to all pupils born in 1936;
(2) completing a short sociological schedule for all pupils born in 1936;
(3) completing a detailed sociological schedule for a random sample consisting of all pupils born on the 1st, 2nd and 3rd day of each month in 1936 and for all twins born in 1936;
(4) testing individually about 1000 pupils by the Terman-Merrill scale to calibrate the group test.

In view of the valuable results which are likely to accrue from this inquiry, the Research Council would be much indebted if you would take a personal interest in the arrangements and make certain that every pupil of the appropriate age (including such physically defective pupils as are capable), in whatever class or division of your school he or she may be placed, takes the test, that it is performed in strict accordance with the instructions accompanying it, and that the appropriate schedules are completed.

1. *General Instructions for Group Intelligence Test*

The group test is intended to be given to all the pupils present on the day of the test who were born in 1936. The object of the survey is to obtain data about the whole distribution of the intelligence of Scottish pupils from one end of the scale to the other. Mentally defective children should not be asked to face the test. Teachers should complete the first page of the test and add a note indicating that the pupil is mentally defective, or otherwise unfit to take the test.

There is no intention whatever of making any comparisons between schools; and teachers can rest assured that the results of no individual pupil, class, school, or small district will be published.

The test proper is preceded by a ten minutes' preliminary practice test, the object of which is to familiarise the pupils with the type of question to be asked in the test proper. As the front page of the preliminary practice test is exactly the same as that of the test proper, the pupils also have practice in filling in their names and the other information required. This should be checked carefully by the teacher. The preliminary practice test should be given on the same morning as the test proper. It should not be returned as it does not count in the results.

The test proper should be given, after a short interval, during the same forenoon as the preliminary practice test. The actual working time is 48 minutes, so that with allowance for distribution and the reading of instructions, about an hour is required, in addition to the time for the preliminary practice test.

The pupils do their work on the pages of the test booklet, in pencil. Each pupil should be supplied with two sharpened pencils and nothing else—no rulers, india-rubber, jotting paper or blotting paper. The pupils should be seated at distances from one another such as are customary in school examinations.

Before distributing the booklets, the supervisor will say: " Do not turn over or open any of these books until you are told." As some of the questions are on the back page, care must be taken to distribute the books right side up. For the distribution of the booklets, for the filling up of the front page (name, etc.), and for settling down, about ten minutes are required, or less in small centres.

As the timing of the tests must be done very exactly, each supervising teacher should see that on the morning of the test he or she is in possession of a *watch with a seconds hand.*

Where possible there should be two supervisors. One will stand at the desk facing the pupils, reading the instructions when necessary, keeping the time with a watch before him, observing that no pupil looks at his neighbour's paper, and generally supervising the whole arrangements. He should not permit himself to be distracted by callers entering the room, by talking to other teachers, by reading the test booklet himself, or by attempting to do work of his own during the period.

The second supervisor should patrol the room quietly and unobtrusively. He should have with him a reserve supply of pencils. Besides watching that no pupil copies, he should be on the alert for any pupil who has not turned to the right page, or has failed to notice that there are questions on the back page, etc. As a rule it will only be obvious blunderers who need a special eye on them, and an indication with the finger or a whispered word of explanation is all that is needed. *Otherwise no assistance is to be given, and no questions whatever are to be answered.*

In small centres one supervisor will be sufficient, though, where possible, a second should be present.

The particular instructions for the tests will be forwarded with the scripts, and should not be opened until the morning of the test, when they should be carefully studied by the supervisor both before giving the preliminary practice test and in the short interval which should be allowed between this and the test proper. They must be exactly followed, and nothing should be said to the pupils in the way of instructions except what is there laid down.

If no instructions are received to the contrary, the completed scripts should be returned to the director of education of your area.

2. *General Instructions for Sociological Schedule*

A sociological schedule must be completed for each child born in 1936. The schedule consists of several simple factual questions regarding the pupil, *e.g.* name, class in school, date

of birth. Practically all the information will be contained on
the pupil's national record card.

The schedules should be completed as soon as possible and
returned to your director of education along with the worked
scripts. It will be helpful if separate parcels are made of the
schedules and of the tests with the pupils' names in alphabetical
order, boys first, and if these are then made into one parcel.

3. *Random-Sample Sociological Schedule*

This schedule should be completed for all pupils born on the 1st,
2nd and 3rd of each month in 1936 and for all twins born in 1936.

The names of the children in the random sample in your
school are on the rolls which you have already completed.
These will be returned to you when the schedules are sent for
completion. In some small schools there are no children in the
random sample and accordingly no random-sample schedules
will be forwarded.

The first 17 questions are identical with those on the ordinary
schedule and should be completed by the teacher: the remainder of the schedule will be completed by investigators appointed by the Research Council. When the first 17 questions
of the random-sample sociological schedules have been completed, these schedules and the roll should be immediately
forwarded to your director of education.

It should be understood that for children in the random
sample two schedules will be completed: (*a*) the Sociological
Schedule which will be completed in full by the teacher and
returned with the worked scripts, and (*b*) the Random-Sample
Sociological Schedule, the first 17 questions of which will also
be completed by the teacher and forwarded to the director of
education, as stated above.

4. *Individual Testing*

The individual testing of about 1000 pupils will be undertaken by qualified testers. If any pupil in your school should
be included in this group, it is hoped that you will afford
facilities for this testing.

All unused tests and schedules must be returned to the Research
Council, along with a note of any expenses incurred for postages.

(*d*) SPECIAL INSTRUCTIONS

The special instructions to the teachers were the same as for
the 1932 survey.[1]

[1] *The Intelligence of Scottish Children*, Appendix I, pp. 127-9.

III

SOCIOLOGICAL INQUIRY

A CONSIDERATION which weighed with the Research Council in overcoming its reluctance to undertake another mental survey was the opportunity the new survey would afford of securing much valuable sociological data. With the experience obtained from the first survey, a repetition on identical lines would have been a comparatively simple undertaking. The sociological aspect, however, complicated the situation, and became, indeed, one of the main preoccupations of the Mental Survey Committee.

SAMPLE

The Committee felt that much valuable information would be gained if certain details regarding the home conditions of the pupils tested could be obtained, with, in addition, a medical history of disease or defect liable to affect intelligence or impair educational attainment. It was obvious that to obtain these data the homes of the children would require to be visited, and in view of the assistance likely to be forthcoming, to carry out this visitation for every eleven-year-old in the country was regarded as an impossible task. The Mental Survey Committee, considering the information required about the child's medical history, was unanimous that the home visitation, to be really effective, would require to be carried out by nurses. It was finally decided that a sample of approximately ten per cent was a suitable one to constitute the sociological and medical inquiry. It was

27

further decided that this group should be representative of the whole country, although it was realised that this decision would add considerably to the difficulties of home visitation compared with the visitation of a sample selected from the more densely populated areas. It was agreed that the sample, referred to as the THIRTY-SIX-DAY SAMPLE, should consist of boys and girls born on the 1st, 2nd and 3rd days of every month in 1936. The same information was also desired for all twins born in 1936. The advantage of this selection of pupils of eleven years of age for home visiting would be that it was quite random and that the group would amount to upwards of 7000 children.

RANDOM-SAMPLE SOCIOLOGICAL SCHEDULE

The type of schedule to be used for this random-sample group had next to be settled, as well as the extent of the sociological and medical information desired. For the purpose of the mental survey of eleven-year-old children in Scotland, a schedule designated the SOCIOLOGICAL SCHEDULE,[1] in which seventeen questions had to be answered, was provided for each pupil. These questions were mainly educational in character and the schedule had to be completed by the child's class teacher. A RANDOM-SAMPLE SOCIOLOGICAL SCHEDULE[2] was also prepared for the seven thousand or so children selected by date of birth, as described above. This schedule contained twenty-five questions, the first seventeen being duplicates of the questions on the general sociological schedule, the remaining eight referring to special sociological and to medical features. The first seventeen questions were intended to be completed by the class teacher before the date of the intelligence test, and the schedules immediately returned to the Research Council, in order

[1] See Appendix I, p. 36.
[2] See Appendix II, p. 38.

that the random-sample inquiry could be started at as early a date as possible.

The questions which appear in the sociological schedule require no explanation, except for question 11, which was intended to reveal whether there were any important recent transferences of population in Scotland. The special sociological and medical questions of the random-sample schedule are given in full below, with a brief comment on the reasons for their inclusion and the information expected from them.

18. *Was child evacuated?*
    (*a*) If so, to which Education Authority?
    (*b*) City, Large town, Small town, Other areas.
    (*c*) For how long (in months)?

It will be obvious that evacuation, if of any duration, would affect a child of tender years very markedly, both emotionally and educationally. The separation from the familiar home circle (particularly from the mother), and the transfer to a foster parent in whose home a different set of values might be operating, might well cause a sense of confusion and unhappiness in any but a stable personality. Similarly a change in scholastic methods might retard the educational progress of the child.

19. *Is child living with his or her own mother?*
The necessity for good parent-child relationship is essential for satisfactory child development, and young children may be adversely affected if they lack the care and supervision of their own mother. Moreover, it was desirable to distinguish between foster children and true children in the home.

20. *Occupation of father or guardian*
This was required in considerable detail in order to assess as closely as possible the social status of the family. The correlation of socio-economic status with grade of

intelligence has frequently been stated in previous investigations, but in this inquiry the range of occupations was made very much wider, and in the occupation the status of the worker was more detailed than usual, in the hope that this would enhance the value of the comparison of social standing with intellectual level.

21. *Date of mother's birth (year only)*

The main reason for this is to distinguish between complete and incomplete families. This, coupled with the number of children in the family, should supply information to assist in answering such questions as:

What is the effect on intelligence of a young mother and a small family?

Is the intelligence of the child of an elderly mother higher than that of the child of a young mother? Or the reverse?

With over seven thousand mothers whose age is known and the place in the family of the eleven-year-old also known, some new information on these and allied matters might well be obtained.

22. *Number of apartments in home*
   Number of individuals in home

The ratio of the one to the other will indicate good or bad living conditions with their presumed good or bad effect on the child.

23. *Height*
24. *Weight*

The relationship of height and weight to mental status is definitely accepted only in children of low mental development, where diminished height and weight compared with normal standards are commonly found. There is, nevertheless, some evidence that a relationship exists between superior intelligence and good physical development. Height and weight may be accepted as reasonably reliable pointers to good physical condition, and the findings of the present mental survey might accordingly supply more definite information on the question of any association of superior intelligence with good physique than has hitherto been available.

25. *Does the child suffer from any of the following physical disabilities ? Congenital Paralysis, Developed Paralysis, Deafness, Epilepsy, Chorea, Defective Vision, Meningitis, Encephalitis (Lethargica or after Infectious Fevers), Defects in Endocrine Glands*

For facility in tabulating the results the disabilities were limited to nine, and were selected because they were regarded as likely to impair intelligence through their direct effect on the central nervous system. Deafness and defective vision were included because children afflicted by these disabilities frequently fail to attain their full educational achievement. Severe diseases such as cardiac, lung, and other general constitutional defects might have their impact on educational attainment indirectly assessed by the frequency of absence from school, or by the attendance of the child at a special school for physically-handicapped children, but no details were asked for constitutional diseases, the numbers of which are, of course, very large. Since the physical defects detailed on the schedule are in the main comparatively rare, and minor endocrine deficiencies are difficult to detect, it is unlikely that, in a group of only seven thousand, many children will be met with who suffer from such defects.

HOME VISITATION

With a random sample of upwards of seven thousand children scattered over the whole country, visitation of their homes presented a problem likely to prove difficult to solve. Contacting the mother to obtain the necessary sociological and medical information was difficult in both town and country. In the town a higher percentage of mothers were in employment, difficulties of shopping caused more protracted absence from the home than under normal conditions, and the staggering of holidays meant more closed homes than usual in the month of June, during which period it was hoped to have the home-visiting of the random-sample cases completed. In the country a serious difficulty was the scattered nature of the population and the inaccessibility of some of the houses.

The incorporation of height and weight in the random-sample schedule brought an additional complication. In most instances, this meant that the nurse, to have access to a weighing machine, would require to visit the school which the child attended, in addition to visiting the home to interview the mother for the other data. This had, however, one considerable advantage. The nurse, when at the school, would have the opportunity of discussing with the child's class teacher any point that her visit to the mother had left in doubt. Further, an opportunity would arise for testing under favourable conditions the hearing and vision of the child, if the acuity of vision or hearing was regarded as unsatisfactory.

Health visitors and district nurses were assumed to be particularly well equipped to carry out the home visitation of the random-sample cases, since their usual duties take them into the people's houses; they have experience in discussing health features with mothers, and the regard in which they are held by mothers would tend to raise to a higher level the number of mothers willing to co-operate than if any other procedure were adopted.

PROCEDURE

Contact by letter was accordingly made with all the medical officers of health of cities and counties in Scotland and with the Queen's Institute of District Nursing, inviting their co-operation in making the home visitation of the thirty-six-day sample a success and emphasizing the importance of the mental survey as a whole. Senior members of the school medical service were also contacted in order to ensure as large a measure of success as possible for the scheme of home visitation. It was pointed out that the various items on the sociological schedule had detailed instructions printed on the schedules and that this would simplify the task of the nurses. The response from the medical officers of health was most gratifying. Medical officers of health all over the country expressed their willingness to enlist the services of the nurses in carrying out the home visitation. Difficulties in respect of home visitation arose on account of delay in receipt of random-sample schedules by medical officers of health. This was occasioned by the demands on teachers to complete an additional schedule for the thirty-six-day sample, by the short time elapsing between the test and the end of the school session, and by the transference of pupils to other schools after the issue of the schedules. It was soon evident that the hope of having home visitation of the thirty-six-day sample completed by the end of June could not be realised. A further letter was sent to medical officers of health with an expression of thanks for the work carried out and an appreciation of the difficulties with which they were faced. Since it was obvious that nothing like the full number of home visitations could be carried out in the month of June, an appeal was made to continue the visitations throughout the summer months. So effectively was this accomplished that the results far exceeded expectations and reflected great credit on the arrangements for home visitation and the enthusiasm and efficiency of the nurses.

The Mental Survey Committee, whilst highly satisfied with the success of the scheme of home visitation, felt that an effort should be made to have as many of the remaining schedules completed as soon as possible, in the hope of achieving a new high level of administrative success. A later date was therefore set for the termination of this effort.

Thereafter, through Dr D. M. McIntosh, who was in charge of the administrative arrangements of the survey, the assistance of school teachers throughout the country was enlisted to tackle cases which for any reason had not been dealt with by the home visitation of the nursing staff.

A letter from the Research Council was sent to all medical officers of health expressing the Council's indebtedness for the co-operation and help given, which had rendered the home visitation of the thirty-six-day sample such a signal success. The Mental Survey Committee asked that an expression of appreciation might be sent to all nurses who had taken part in the scheme of home visitation, as well as to all other members of staff who had participated in the work, emphasizing the highly satisfactory results which had accrued from their efforts.

GEOGRAPHICAL DISTRIBUTION

The number of schedules completed in the different areas for both grant-aided and private schools was as follows:

Area	Thirty-six-Day Sample	Twins in Thirty-six-Day Sample	Other Twins in Age Group
Aberdeen City	239	2	20
Dundee	271	4	46
Edinburgh	643	20	115
Glasgow	1,690	18	185
Aberdeen County	228	2	32
Angus	133	2	30
Argyll	74	—	8
Ayr	484	2	69
Banff	90	—	6

Area	Thirty-six-Day Sample	Twins in Thirty-six-Day Sample	Other Twins in Age Group
Berwick	16	—	4
Bute	19	—	2
Caithness	31	2	5
Clackmannan	48	—	2
Dumfries	133	—	2
Dunbarton	207	2	33
East Lothian	76	4	8
Fife	391	10	66
Inverness	110	—	31
Kincardine	36	2	10
Kirkcudbright	48	—	4
Lanark	813	14	124
Midlothian	159	4	8
Moray and Nairn	86	—	6
Orkney	29	2	2
Peebles	18	—	2
Perth and Kinross	153	2	16
Renfrew	441	—	55
Ross and Cromarty	74	4	10
Roxburgh	54	—	10
Selkirk	20	—	6
Stirling	254	1	26
Sutherland	22	—	2
West Lothian	108	6	12
Wigtown	59	—	4
Zetland	20	—	6
	7,277	103	967

Thirty-six-Day Sample. There were in addition 14 pupils in private schools which refused to co-operate, 14 whose names had been omitted from the rolls and who did not sit the group test, and 4, children of hawkers, tinkers and show people, who could not be reached.

Twin Sample. Information was refused for 6 twins, and 1 was omitted from the roll and absent from the group test.

APPENDICES

Letters to medical officers of health and guide to nurses are appended to this chapter.

APPENDIX I

MENTAL SURVEY 1947

SOCIOLOGICAL SCHEDULE

1. Education Authority ....

2. Full name of School (in block capitals) ....

   (a) Official Number of School ....

3. City, Large town, Small town, Other areas ....

   Cities are: Aberdeen, Dundee, Edinburgh, Glasgow.

   Large Towns (Population over 20,000 at 1931 Census): Airdrie, Ayr, Clydebank, Coatbridge, Dumbarton, Dumfries, Dunfermline, Falkirk, Greenock, Hamilton, Inverness, Kilmarnock, Kirkcaldy, Motherwell and Wishaw, Paisley, Perth, Rutherglen, Stirling.

   Small Towns (Population less than 20,000 but over 10,000 at 1931 Census): Alloa, Arbroath, Barrhead, Bathgate, Borrowstounness, Buckhaven and Methil, Cowdenbeath, Galashiels, Grangemouth, Hawick, Irvine, Johnstone, Kirkintilloch, Montrose, Musselburgh, Peterhead, Port-Glasgow, Renfrew, Saltcoats.

4. Size of School: Average number of pupils on roll at 16th May, including all departments and classes ....

5. Number of all full-time teachers at 16th May, including Headmaster and Infant Mistress but not visiting teachers ....

6. Surname of pupil (in block capitals) ....

   Full Christian names (in block capitals) ....

7. Home address ....

   (a) City, Large town, Small town, Other areas ....

8. Class in school ....

   In a one-teacher school or where the number of pupils in the school is so small that there is limitation of classes, the teacher might endeavour, by consideration of the pupil's educational attainments, to determine the class for which he would be fitted

E

9. Date of birth: Day.................. Month.................. Year..................

10. Sex {M..................
       {F.................. (Mark by X)

11. Place of residence of parents when child was born..................

    (a) Is child living in (or near) his birthplace? Answer Yes or No..................

12. Position in family (expressed as fraction)..................

    Fractions to be used, $\frac{1}{1}$, $\frac{1}{3}$, $\frac{4}{7}$, i.e. the only child, eldest of three, fourth of seven. Only full brothers and sisters now alive should be reckoned. If the child has a twin, the earlier of the two possible positions in the family should be shown. For example, if the second and third children of a family of five are twins, each of the twins should be recorded as $\frac{2}{5}$, the fourth child being recorded as $\frac{4}{5}$. Similarly, for triplets the earliest of the three possible positions in family should be given.

13. Has child a twin taking this test?   If so, give name..................
    and school.

14. Has child a brother or sister, other than ....
    a twin, born in 1936? If so, give ....
    name, date of birth and school.

15. Attendances during session 1946-47 to 16th May.   (a) Actual:..................
                                                         (b) Possible:..................

16. Number of schools previously attended..................
    If the same school has been attended twice this counts as two schools. Promotion from one division to another, even when it involves a change of building, is not to be counted as a change of school, nor are Nursery Schools to be counted.

17. Has this pupil been previously tested by a group
    intelligence test during session 1946-47?

9.

10.

11.
(a)

12.

13.

14.

15.
(a)
15.
(b)

15.
(c)

16.

17.

P   V

Serial
Number

APPENDIX II

MENTAL SURVEY 1947

RANDOM - SAMPLE SOCIOLOGICAL SCHEDULE

This schedule is for children born on the 1st, 2nd and 3rd days of each month and for all twins born in 1936.

FOR OFFICE USE ONLY

1. Education Authority ....

2. Full name of School (in block capitals)..

    (*a*) Official Number of School................................

3. City, Large town, Small town, Other areas...............................

    Cities are: Aberdeen, Dundee, Edinburgh, Glasgow.

    Large Towns (Population over 20,000 at 1931 Census): Airdrie, Ayr, Clydebank, Coatbridge, Dumbarton, Dumfries, Dunfermline, Falkirk, Greenock, Hamilton, Inverness, Kilmarnock, Kirkcaldy, Motherwell and Wishaw, Paisley, Perth, Rutherglen, Stirling.

    Small Towns (Population less than 20,000 but over 10,000 at 1931 Census): Alloa, Arbroath, Barrhead, Bathgate, Borrowstounness, Buckhaven and Methil, Cowdenbeath, Galashiels, Grangemouth, Hawick, Irvine, Johnstone, Kirkintilloch, Montrose, Musselburgh, Peterhead, Port-Glasgow, Renfrew, Saltcoats.

4. Size of School: Average number of pupils on roll at 16th May, including all departments and classes.............

5. Number of all full-time teachers at 16th May, including Headmaster and Infant Mistress but not visiting teachers...............................

6. Surname of pupil (in block capitals)..................................

    Full Christian names (in block capitals)...............................

1.

2. (a)

2. (b)

3.

4.

5.

5. (a)

7. Home address ....
   (a) City, Large town, Small town, Other areas ....

8. Class in school ....
   In a one-teacher school or where the number of pupils in the school is so small that there is limitation of classes, the teacher might endeavour, by consideration of the pupil's educational attainments, to determine the class for which he would be fitted under more normal school conditions, e.g. Primary III, etc.

9. Date of birth: Day.............. Month.............. Year..............

10. Sex {M.............. (Mark by X)
        {F..............

11. Place of residence of parents when child was born..............
    (a) Is child living in (or near) his birthplace? Answer Yes or No. ....

12. Position in family (expressed as fraction)..............
    Fractions to be used, $\frac{1}{1}$, $\frac{1}{3}$, $\frac{4}{7}$, i.e. the only child, eldest of three, fourth of seven. Only full brothers and sisters now alive should be reckoned. If the child has a twin, the earlier of the two possible positions in the family should be shown. For example, if the second and third children of a family of five are twins, each of the twins should be recorded as $\frac{2}{5}$, the fourth child being recorded as $\frac{4}{5}$. Similarly, for triplets, the earliest of the three possible positions in family should be given.

13. Has child a twin taking this test? If so, give name..............
    and school ....

FOR OFFICE USE ONLY

2

14. Has child a brother or sister, other than a twin, born in 1936? If so, give name, date of birth and school. ....

14. ☐

15. Attendances during session 1946-47 to 16th May. (a) Actual: ....

(b) Possible: ....

15. (a) ☐

15. (b) ☐

15. (c) ☐

16. Number of schools previously attended ....
    If the same school has been attended twice this counts as two schools. Promotion from one division to another, even when it involves a change of building, is not to be counted as a change of school, nor are Nursery Schools to be counted.

16. ☐

17. Has this pupil been previously tested by a group intelligence test during session 1946-47? ....

17. ☐

18. Was child evacuated? ....

(a) If so, to which Education Authority? ....

(b) City, Large town, Small town, Other areas ....

(c) For how long (in months)? ....

18. ☐

18. (a) ☐

18. (b) ☐

18. (c) ☐

19. Is child living with his or her own mother? ....

19. ☐

20. **Occupation of father or guardian**

(a) Describe below the KIND of work done by the father or guardian in as much detail as possible; for example, if he is an engineer, say EXACTLY what kind of engineer.

If he is retired, out of work, or dead, state his former *customary* occupation—do *not* say " old age pensioner ". If he was killed while serving temporarily in the Forces, the answer should state his occupation before he went into the Forces.

If he is temporarily in the Armed Forces— state former occupation. If no former occupation —put " Armed Forces ".

If he is a regular Sailor, Soldier or Airman—state which and give his rank.

(a) ....

(b) Is the parent or guardian

(1) An employer of 10 or more people?

or

(2) Working for himself or employing LESS than 10 people?

or

(3) Employed and earning a monthly salary?

or

(4) Employed and earning a weekly or other wage?

Put a ring round the number which applies.

(c) Employer's Business (if the parent or guardian is *not* himself an employer or working for himself).

(c) ....

20. ☐

3

Remember that it will not be possible to make an accurate assessment of the family's social class unless this question is answered fully and in detail.

Bearing the above qualifications in mind, you should see that the answers to parts (a) and (b) of Question 20 are in full detail. This is particularly important as regards Question 20(a). Thus, you should not accept an answer such as "engineer", "civil servant", "local government employee", "miner", "labourer", or any similar very broad description. You should ask the parent in such cases to tell you what kind of engineer (and whether professionally qualified), what rank in the civil service or in local government service, what kind of miner and doing exactly what kind of work in the mine, what type of labourer and so forth. In addition, if a father is described as a "manager" of a concern, you should try to find out (and record on the form) whether he is a manager of the concern as a whole, or a branch manager of one part of the concern—for example, a branch manager of a store in a chain-store organisation.

The following examples will give our idea of the type of detail desirable:—

CLERKS: Solicitor's Managing Clerk, Builder's Estimating Clerk, Railway Clerk.

ENGINEERING AND METAL TRADES: Loom Fitter, Textile Engineers; Pneumatic Driller, Shipbuilding; Brass Caster, Lighting Fittings; Press Stamp Operator, Aluminium Hollowware; Girder Plater, Constructional Engineering; Steel Furnaceman, Steel Rolling Mill; Iron Foundry Furnaceman; Locomotive Erector; Master Blacksmith.

FARMING: Market Gardener (Own Account); Dairy Farmer; Farm Carter; Cowman; Horseman on Farm.

LABOURERS: Riveter's Labourer, Shipyard; Permanent Way Labourer; Public Works Contractor's Labourer; Wharf Labourer; Iron Foundry Labourer; General Labourer, Brickworks; Coal Hoist Labourer; Fitter's Labourer, Motor Works.

TEXTILE OPERATIVES: Head Carder, Cotton Spinning; Fly Frame Tenter, Cotton Spinning; Artificial Silk Spinner; Overlooker, Hosiery Manufacturers.

GENERAL: Confectioner (Cake Maker); Confectioner (Sugar Confectionery Manufacturers); Wholesale Meat Salesman (Master); Tailor (Master); Butcher (Shopkeeper); Silk Merchant.

Question 20(b) is not difficult to understand and should not be difficult to answer.

You should remember the following points:—

(i) The term salary (item 3) includes all salaries, monthly, quarterly and up-wards, and relates to employees.

(ii) The term wage covers people who are wage earners and who receive their pay weekly, daily or at other intervals shorter than a month.

On no account, however, should you ask what is the father's income.

Question 20(c), which relates to employees and wage earners, asks for a statement of the employer's business or industry, and is straightforward. For example, if a man is a shop assistant, Question 20(c) should be answered by stating the nature of the shop or other concern for which he works—*i.e.* drapery shop, department store, etc.

21. Date of mother's birth (year only)...................

22. Number of apartments in home...................

To include kitchen but not bathroom.

Number of individuals in home...................

All individuals permanently resident in the home, including any temporarily absent in the Armed Forces.

23. Height...................inches

24. Weight...................lbs.

Height and Weight. This should be taken to the nearest completed half inch and half pound; a statistical correction will be made for the additional height and weight. Children's height should be taken in their stocking soles, feet together, erect, and with the head able to move comfortably under the sliding measuring rod. Weight should be taken with shoes off and stripped to the waist to achieve a reasonable degree of uniformity of standard. Weighing machines should be tested prior to weighing to ensure that they are registering accurately.

Date when taken...................

25.

P

V

M

C — Individual testing

Q

Serial number

4

25. Does the child suffer from any of the following physical disabilities (check items in list)?

Disease	Mark with X
Congenital Paralysis	
Developed Paralysis	
Deafness	
Epilepsy	
Chorea	
Defective Vision	
Meningitis	
Encephalitis { Lethargica or after / Infectious Fevers	
Defects in Endocrine Glands, *e.g.* thyroid, pituitary	

Guide to Ascertainment of Detailed Physical Disability.

(1) *Congenital Paralysis.* It is important to know if a paralysis is congenital, as in this form there is frequently an accompanying destruction of nerve cells in the brain with a consequent mental impairment. Inquiry at the mother should be directed as to child's movements during infancy and the age at which walking commenced. It should not be difficult to decide in most cases that the paralysis is one of birth.

(Infantile Paralysis); T.B. of the spine and other less common conditions can cause paralysis. Pupils wearing casts or irons in the treatment of T.B. joints are not to be regarded as suffering from paralysis.

(3) *Deafness.* Generally, there will not be much difficulty in obtaining from parents information about deafness, although minor degrees may be passed over by parents as lack of attention on the child's part. Should there be doubt and the child is present, a reasonably accurate test is as follows: Stand the child approximately 20 feet away with his back turned, and ask him to repeat certain numbers. Ears can be tested separately by putting a finger in the ear not tested at the time. A loud whisper should be heard at 20 feet in quiet surroundings.

(4) *Epilepsy.* There is usually no difficulty in assessing this condition.

(5) *Chorea.* This should be noted if the child has had chorea at any time. Confusion must be avoided with Habit Spasm, which is a repetition of one or more muscular movements and not the widespread involuntary movements of chorea. If the child has not been confined to bed for a month or six weeks or admitted to hospital, it is unlikely to be chorea.

(6) *Defective Vision.* An accurate return of this will be difficult. Children whose error of refraction has been satisfactorily corrected by spectacles are not to be classed as suffering from defective vision. If spectacles have been supplied and are not worn (as so often happens) the child should be stated to have defective vision.

(7) *Meningitis.* Careful inquiry should elicit if the child has had meningitis. Parents often speak of their children being threatened with meningitis.

(8) *Encephalitis (Lethargica or after Infectious Fevers).* This will occur but rarely. A minor form of paralysis after Scarlet Fever, Mumps, Measles, etc., particularly if associated with a deterioration in school work, would indicate Encephalitis after Fevers.

(9) *Endocrine Defects.* This will usually be a sub-thyroid or more rarely cretin. Some pituitary defects may be met with.

By whom was schedule completed?

Name (Mr, Mrs, Miss)..

Designation (*e.g.* Health Visitor)..

Address..

Investigators should make it clear that participation in the Survey is purely optional.

APPENDIX III

(a) LETTER TO MEDICAL OFFICERS OF HEALTH

The Scottish Council for Research in Education, after considerable hesitation, has agreed to the request of the Population Investigation Committee to undertake a group mental survey similar to that conducted in 1932, in order to secure evidence for the Royal Commission on Population to determine whether or not there has been any decline in intelligence in the interval between the two surveys.

All eleven-year-old children in Scotland will be tested in June of this year. Of this group a sample is to be selected which will be subjected to a more detailed investigation; the numbers of the random sample for the whole country will amount to a maximum of 7,200. This sample will be spread over the whole country proportionate to the population of the different areas.

A schedule has been prepared, a copy of which is enclosed for your information. You will observe that most of the information requested will be supplied by the school teacher, but that certain items are of a purely medical nature. In view of this, the Research Council felt that by far the most suitable person to visit the home to obtain the necessary information would be the school nurse, health visitor or district nurse, and the Council would be most grateful for your help in this matter.

Should you be agreeable to the health visitors carrying out the home visitation, their inquiries would be limited to obtaining information on (1) the physical condition of the child, as detailed in the schedule, the nine items having been selected on account of their effect on the mental development of the pupil; (2) date of mother's birth, or, if not available, age of mother; (3) number of apartments and number of persons in the home.

Some notes are attached as a guide in assessing the physical defects enumerated.

As this investigation is directed to the eleven-year-old group of school children, the medical schedules in schools will not provide the necessary information. The nearest age at which routine inspection is carried out in the schools is nine years, whilst, in addition, there was a great reduction in the examination of nine-year-olds on account of curtailment during the war years.

The Research Council would esteem it a favour if you could see your way to inform them at your early convenience whether you can enlist the co-operation of the health visitors in your area in the directions indicated above.

(b) Extracts from Letter to Medical Officers of Health

. . . The medical and sociological information, particularly in regard to the father's occupation, is requested in considerable detail, but full explanatory notes are incorporated in the schedule. The Council, whilst aware of the wide occupational range demanded, felt this to be desirable, since in the Royal Commission on Population Family Census such information was asked for in this form.

Health visitors and school and district nurses carrying out home visitation will fill in the schedules from question 18 to the end.

It will be observed that height and weight have to be taken. While it is agreed that this factor is an additional complication, the Council felt that, when children, during weighing, were stripped to the waist, it was a job for a nurse rather than for a teacher. There is, however, a definite advantage in the nurse's visit to the school. If there is any doubt about the medical information, the class teacher should be consulted, as her opinion will be invaluable. In addition, a special opportunity is available for testing hearing and vision (which could not be done otherwise), since in almost all schools there will be a sight-testing card.

In view of the admitted detailed nature of some of the questions, the Council would be grateful if medical officers, where possible, would discuss the schedules with the nurses concerned, in order to reduce the risk of error to a minimum. Should this not be possible, intimation of visits to homes might be accompanied by as full explanatory details as possible.

. . . Nurses will, of course, receive travelling expenses and the refund of any reasonable outlay on food and refreshments during the course of the home visitation.

The Council would be grateful if you would do all you can to make this survey a success, and wherever possible, to enlist the full co-operation of medical officers and nurses to further this end.

(c) GUIDE TO NURSES

A mental survey of eleven-year-old children is to be carried out in all Scottish schools on 4th June 1947.

This inquiry is arousing the greatest interest not only in this country but also abroad. Many important features in regard to the intellectual development of children will be derived from it.

Associated with this scheme, the Scottish Council for Research in Education has selected a smaller group for special investigation into social conditions in the home and their medical history. Considerable importance is attached to this information. These random-sample pupils are selected by date of birth and are a representative group for the whole of Scotland. Children born on the 1st, 2nd and 3rd days of the months in 1936 and all twins born in 1936 comprise the group.

The information required is simple, although the schedule appears somewhat formidable, but this is due to the fact that detailed instructions are given as to the answering of the various questions. This is particularly noticeable in the answering of question 20—father's occupation. Nurses will fill in this schedule commencing at question 18. Questions 1-17 should have been filled in by the school teachers.

It would be an advantage if nurses, before filling in the schedules, would acquaint themselves fully with the instructions, since, if these detailed instructions are completely understood, the answering of the questions will be simple. An additional visit will be required. Height and weight have to be taken and comment made on any defect of vision or hearing. This will necessitate a visit to the school for the purpose, where there will probably be a weighing machine, but in addition, contact with the teacher may be of value for getting information about hearing, vision, or medical history, should the parent not have full given details.

IV

INDIVIDUAL TESTING

SELECTION OF A REPRESENTATIVE SAMPLE

IN the 1932 mental survey of the children born in 1921 a not too successful attempt was made by a combination of proportional geographical distribution and approximate date of birth to obtain a random representative sample of a thousand pupils for individual testing. In the present survey the committee resolved to adhere strictly to the date of birth as the basis of selection. In order to obtain a sample of at least a thousand pupils it was considered advisable to select children born on six days in the year. Since a thirty-six-day sample had already been made of all children born on the first three days of each month for the more detailed sociological survey, six of these days, the first of the " even months "—February, April, June, August, October and December—were chosen as dates of birth for individual testing.

THE TEST

In the 1932 survey the Stanford (1916) Revision of the Binet-Simon scale, suitably modified for Scottish children, was used for the individual testing, but for a variety of reasons the committee decided to use for the present survey the L form of the Terman-Merrill (1937) Revision, with the Scottish modifications proposed by the Scottish Research Council.[1] This will facilitate any

[1] *The Terman-Merrill Intelligence Scale in Scotland* by D. Kennedy-Fraser. Publications of the Scottish Council for Research in Education, XXIII. London: The University of London Press, Ltd., 1945.

later comparison by means of the currently used individual test. For calibration purposes it was decided to apply both tests to some children of the age group (see Appendix I, p. 59).

THE TESTERS

The task of testing over twelve hundred children scattered all over the country with no full-time testers available would have daunted even such an incurable optimist as the writer, had it not been for the keen co-operation of a large and ever willing group of colleagues and students. Under his general direction the Aberdeen region was organised by Dr Walker of Aberdeen University, the Dundee region by Miss Young of the Dundee Training College, and the Edinburgh region by Miss Thomson of Moray House Training College.[1] In some of the counties the directors of education undertook personal responsibility, and in the ever increasing number of cities and counties with educational psychologists on their staffs, these officials took complete and efficient charge. In one county the testing was undertaken by former students of the writer under the supervision of two of the head masters. The rest of the country was covered by the writer and his friends, mainly during their holidays. All the testers were carefully selected on the basis of their training and experience.

[1] Thanks are also due to those who undertook testing in the following areas: Aberdeen, Messrs H. McRae, A. Laing, J. Turnbull, Misses D. M. Forster and R. J. Garden; Dundee, Mr G. W. Sturrock; Edinburgh, Miss A. T. Paterson and Mr D. S. Petrie; Glasgow, Miss C. M. McCallum and staff, and Miss V. M. McLaren; Aberdeenshire, Mr A. L. Young; Argyll, Mr A. M. Orr; Ayrshire, Mr L. Duncan; Banff, Mr J. McNaught; Clackmannanshire, Mr A. C. Marshall; Dumfriesshire-Wigtownshire, Miss M. Martin; Dunbartonshire, Miss I. A. Buchanan; East Lothian, Dr J. Meiklejohn; Fife, Miss I. C. Maclean; Lanarkshire, Mr T. Smith; Midlothian, Mr Wallace; Perthshire, Mr D. Howat; Renfrewshire, Messrs A. A. L. Brodie and W. L. McKinlay; Ross-shire, Mr J. A. Smith; Zetland, Mr J. H. Spence.

DATE OF TESTING

It was originally intended to complete the testing within six months, three months before and three months after the group test on 4th June, but owing to delays in the marking of the group-test scripts and the consequent notification of missing cases, the individual testing was still incomplete by the beginning of April 1948. It was felt, however, that the higher proportion of the whole group thus tested more than compensated for the delay in completing the testing.

CHRONOLOGICAL AGE OF CHILDREN

In spite of this unexpected extension of the period of testing, the chronological ages of the children, with two exceptions, at the date of individual testing ranged from only 10 years 2 months to 12 years 1 month, with the median at 11 years and the quartiles at 10 years 9 months and 11 years 2 months. Thus the group as a whole consists mainly of eleven-year-old children.

DISTRIBUTION OF CHRONOLOGICAL AGES

C.A. in years and months		All	Boys	Girls
11.11	-	12.1	9	5	4
11.8	-	11.10	37	26	11
11.5	-	11.7	71	38	33
11.2	-	11.4	292	138	154
10.11	-	11.1	346	176	170
10.8	-	10.10	246	112	134
10.5	-	10.7	198	93	105
10.2	-	10.4	14	6	8
*8.10	-	8.11	2	1	1

* The IQs of two pupils in special schools were known, and it was considered inadvisable to re-test them.

THE SIX-DAY SAMPLE

A preliminary scrutiny of the nominal rolls of the thirty-six-day sample revealed an apparent total of 1,171 pupils born on the six days, but when the testers came to follow up these cases, twenty-one were found not actually to have been born on these dates. Finally, when the group scripts came and were checked, an additional eighty " even-month " pupils were found. Thus the actual sample consisted of 1,230 pupils, of whom 1,215[1] were tested individually; ninety-five (7·82%)[2] of the 1,215 pupils were absent from the group test; this leaves 1,120 whose individual IQs and group scores can be compared. The results from this group are dealt with in Chapter VI (pp. 94-6), Chapter VII (pp. 113-4), and Chapter VIII.

GEOGRAPHICAL ANALYSIS

While no figures are published for the separate cities and counties, the data have been separated into those for the four cities—Aberdeen, Dundee, Edinburgh and Glasgow—and those for the rest of the country—thirty-one counties—and also for the sexes and months of birth.

Any further geographical sub-classification was based on the location of the school attended by the pupil and not by his place of birth or home. Thus any bright child coming in from the surrounding counties to one of the city schools was classified as a city child; a pupil born

[1] Only fifteen (1·2%) of the children in the six-day sample were not given an individual test, and of these, five were in schools where their teachers or their parents refused permission for the test to be applied, two were in hospital medically unfit, four were in relatively inaccessible islands, and four (including one tinker's boy with a group score of P:2, V:0) kept changing so rapidly from school to school and even from county to county that they could not be reached. The group-test scores of thirteen of these missing pupils were 59, 54, 54, 47, 40, 34, 31, 26, 22, 20, 6, 3 and 0, with a mean score of 30·46 as compared with a mean score of 37·27 for the 1,120 children who were individually tested and who took the group test. All but one of these pupils were in the counties group. After the tabulation was completed and the calculations made, an additional child was reported. She was a low-grade idiot quite incapable of responding to tests.

[2] The Terman-Merrill IQs of these ninety-five pupils are given in Appendix II, p. 61.

in England and attending a school in the north of Scotland was classified with the north-country children; and a boarded-out child from a Clydeside industrial town was classified with the rural children in the one-class school she was attending. A child born in Scotland in 1936 and now attending a school elsewhere was, naturally, not included.

Table I shows the geographical distribution of

(1) pupils aged 11 and under 12 on 31st July 1947, estimated by the Scottish Education Department, and reduced to 1,215;
(2) the six-day sample of 1,215 who were individually tested;
(3) the individually-tested children born in 1921;
(4) the individually-tested children born in 1926.

RESULTS

In Appendix III, p. 62, are listed the Terman-Merrill intelligence quotients and the group verbal scores of the 1,215 pupils of the six-day sample grouped by sex, by date of birth and by geographical area of school attended (four cities and thirty-one counties) in rank order of IQ. Calculations from these data give the following figures:

	All	Boys	Girls	Cities	Counties
Number	1,215	595	620	471	744
Mean IQ	102·523	104·387	100·734	104·943	100·991
Standard Deviation	20·056	19·923	20·012	19·645	20·163

Thus for this particular six-day sample the mean IQ of all pupils is significantly superior to 100; the boys' mean IQ is also significantly superior to 100, but that of the girls is not. The boys' mean IQ is significantly superior to that of the girls (difference is 3·24 times the standard error),[1] and the mean IQ of the city pupils is

[1] In *The Intelligence of Scottish Children* (p. 93), the significance of the differences was assessed from the " probable error " and not from the " standard error ".

F

TABLE I
Geographical Distribution

	*Department's Estimate	Six-Day Sample			Binet Thousand			Macmeeken Representative Sample		
	1947	1947			1932			1937		
	All	All	Boys	Girls	All	Boys	Girls	All	Boys	Girls
Cities—										
Aberdeen	44	39	18	21	23	14	9	25	10	15
Dundee	44	35	17	18	37	19	18	33	17	16
Edinburgh	101	113	51	62	92	40	52	76	42	34
Glasgow	275	284	141	143	231	116	115	185	90	95
Total	464	471	227	244	383	189	194	319	159	160
Counties—										
Aberdeen	37	37	16	21	14	10	4	37	23	14
Angus	21	19	10	9	17	8	9	9	6	3
Argyll	14	10	5	5	10	6	4	10	4	6
Ayr	77	77	37	40	65	35	30	60	27	33
Banff	16	11	5	6	12	7	5	7	5	2
Berwick	4	3	1	2	5	2	3	0	0	0
Bute	4	0	0	0	5	2	3	4	4	0
Caithness	6	5	2	3	0	0	0	3	2	1
Clackmannan	9	6	3	3	8	4	4	9	6	3
Dumfries	20	17	10	7	18	9	9	12	6	6
Dunbarton	34	36	19	17	30	16	14	34	18	16
East Lothian	12	16	8	8	6	3	3	12	5	7
Fife	70	70	34	36	62	30	32	47	25	22
Inverness	20	17	10	7	10	5	5	13	7	6
Kincardine	6	5	3	2	6	5	1	4	0	4
Kirkcudbright	8	8	2	6	8	4	4	9	7	2
Lanark	139	133	67	66	132	60	72	107	49	58
Midlothian	22	23	12	11	19	10	9	18	12	6
Moray & Nairn	13	21	11	10	9	5	4	2	1	1
Orkney	5	1	1	0	4	4	0	4	2	2
Peebles	3	4	1	3	0	0	0	2	1	1
Perth & Kinross	28	25	15	10	23	12	11	19	10	9
Renfrew	77	83	34	49	52	24	28	46	29	17
Ross & Cromarty	13	13	6	7	8	4	4	8	4	4
Roxburgh	9	8	4	4	8	4	4	6	4	2
Selkirk	4	6	2	4	4	4	0	2	2	0
Stirling	44	48	29	19	33	16	17	41	16	25
Sutherland	3	2	2	0	3	2	1	2	1	1
West Lothian	22	27	12	15	23	12	11	19	7	12
Wigtown	7	9	4	5	19	6	13	6	2	4
Zetland	4	4	3	1	4	2	2	3	0	3
Total	751	744	368	376	617	311	306	555	285	270
Whole Country	1,215	1,215	595	620	1,000	500	500	874	444	430

* The Department's figures refer to a slightly different calendar year and apply only to pupils on the registers of grant-aided schools.

also significantly superior to the mean of the pupils in the counties (difference is 3·38 times the standard error).

Similar results were obtained from the actual IQs ascertained with the 1000 individually-tested children born in 1921,[1] but closer scrutiny of the data and comparison of the verbal scores of that sample with those of the age group seemed to indicate caution in accepting the results as they stood. In the present survey one element of possible bias in sampling has been removed by the rigid adherence to six definite dates of birth of the pupils tested individually.

MEANS
Calculated for all the 1,215 Children direct from Individual IQs

Date of Survey	Test Used	Date of Birth	All N	M_{IQ}	Boys N	M_{IQ}	Girls N	M_{IQ}
1947	Terman-Merrill (1937)	1936	1,215	102·523	595	104·387	620	100·734
1937	Stanford (1916)	1926	874	100·11	444	100·51	430	99·70
1932	Stanford (1916)	1921	1,000	101·6	500	103·0	500	100·2

VARIABILITY

			N	S.D.	N	S.D.	N	S.D.
1947	Terman-Merrill (1937)	1936	1,215	20·056	595	19·923	620	20·012
1937	Stanford (1916)	1926	874	15·58	444	15·88	430	15·24
1932	Stanford (1916)	1921	1,000	16·77	500	17·34	500	16·1

If the standard deviation (S.D. or σ) is employed as the measure of variation, it appears from the data of the six-day sample of 1,215 pupils born in 1936 that the Terman-Merrill L scale yields a higher standard deviation of 20 points for all children and for boys and girls separately when compared with standard deviations of 17 for boys and 16 for girls when the Stanford (1916) Revision was used with Scottish children born in 1921. It is interesting to note that Terman and Merrill[2] suggest standard devia-

[1] *The Intelligence of Scottish Children*, p. 93.
[2] L. M. Terman and M. A. Merrill, *Measuring Intelligence*. New York: Houghton Mifflin Company, 1937. London: George G. Harrap & Co. Ltd., 1937. P. 40.

tions of 18 for eleven-year-olds and 20 for twelve-year-olds. Thus our present mainly eleven-year-old group of Scottish children appears to be distributed as widely as the American twelve-year-old group.

IQ Variability in Relation to Age for American Children

Test used	Age	N	S.D.
Terrman-Merrill (1937)	10 years	201	16·5
	11 „	204	18·0
	12 „	202	20·0
Stanford (1916)		905	13·0

As another means of estimating the spread of the different groups we can compare the percentages of children in five groups with IQ class limits of 130, 110, 90 and 70. Table II shows these percentages for the 1947 and 1932 surveys, which, without correction for the greater standard deviation, indicate considerable differences between the 1936 and 1921 Scottish children. McNemar[1] has, however, indicated the adjustments necessary in IQs obtained by the Terman-Merrill Revision with a standard deviation of 20 to equate them to the smaller standard deviation of the earlier Stanford Revision; IQs 134, 112, 88 and 66 on the Terman-Merrill with a σ of 20 are, when so adjusted, equivalent to 130, 110, 90 and 70 on the Stanford. With these as our class limits we obtain a percentage distribution as given in column 1936*, which corresponds more closely to the distribution found in the 1932 survey.

INFLUENCE OF MONTH OF BIRTH

The influence, if any, of month of birth on the IQ can be deduced from the data in Table III. The descending monthly order of mean IQs for all pupils is April, June, February, October, August and December.

[1] McNemar, *The Revision of the Stanford Binet Scale.* New York: Houghton Mifflin Company, 1942. London: George G. Harrap & Co. Ltd., 1942. P. 173, Table 52.

TABLE II
Percentage at Different Levels of Intelligence
for the Geographical Areas
Comparison of Results for Pupils born in 1936 and 1921

All

IQ	All Pupils born in			Boys born in			Girls born in		
	1936	1936*	1921	1936	1936*	1921	1936	1936*	1921
Above 129	10·0	(6·8)	6·1	10·8	(7·6)	6·2	9·4	(6·1)	6·0
110–129	22·8	(22·6)	23·5	25·0	(24·5)	26·8	20·7	(20·7)	20·2
90–109	39·9	(46·5)	44·8	41·3	(47·4)	43·2	38·5	(45·6)	46·4
70–89	24·3	(22·7)	25·0	20·5	(19·3)	23·2	27·9	(26·0)	26·8
Below 70	3·0	(1·4)	0·6	2·4	(1·2)	0·6	3·5	(1·6)	0·6
Number	1,215		1,000	595		500	620		500
Mean	102·523		101·46	104·387		102·74	100·734		100·17
S.D.	20·056		16·77	19·923		17·34	20·01		16·1

Cities

IQ	All Pupils born in			Boys born in			Girls born in		
Above 129	11·9	(7·9)*	6·5	12·3	(7·5)*	7·8	11·5	(8·2)*	5·9
110–129	24·0	(24·2)	25·6	26·0	(27·8)	31·3	22·1	(20·9)	19·3
90–109	42·3	(49·2)	47·5	45·0	(49·8)	44·8	39·8	(48·8)	50·1
70–89	20·8	(18·3)	20·4	16·3	(14·9)	16·1	25·0	(21·3)	24·7
Below 70	1·0	(0·4)	0·0	0·4	(0·0)	0·0	1·6	(0·8)	0·0
Number	471		383	227		189	244		194
Mean	104·943		103·73	106·69		105·93	103·32		101·59
S.D.	19·645		15·11	19·09		16·72	20·00		16·24

Counties

IQ	All Pupils born in			Boys born in			Girls born in		
Above 129	8·9	(6·2)*	5·7	9·8	(7·6)*	5·1	8·0	(4·8)*	6·1
110–129	22·0	(21·5)	22·4	24·5	(22·6)	24·0	19·7	(20·5)	20·7
90–109	38·5	(44·8)	43·1	39·1	(45·9)	42·3	37·8	(43·6)	44·3
70–89	26·5	(25·5)	27·9	23·1	(22·0)	27·7	29·8	(29·0)	28·0
Below 70	4·1	(2·0)	0·9	3·5	(1·9)	0·9	4·8	(2·1)	0·9
Number	744		617	368		311	376		306
Mean	100·991		100·05	102·97		100·80	99·05		99·28
S.D.	20·163		16·63	20·32		16·53	19·84		13·90

* In columns 1936* the figures in brackets indicate the percentages within the various IQ limits when the larger standard deviation of the Terman-Merrill is equated to the standard deviation of the Stanford Revision; thus 10 per cent of the pupils born in 1936 and tested individually have on the Terman-Merrill Revision, with a σ of 20, IQs over 129, whereas, with the same σ as the earlier Stanford Revision (17 for boys and 16 for girls), only 6·8 would have IQs over 129.

TABLE III

IQs GROUPED BY MONTH OF BIRTH AND SEX FOR CITIES, COUNTIES AND WHOLE COUNTRY

SIX-DAY SAMPLE (1947)—TERMAN-MERRILL REVISION

	Cities			Counties			Whole Country		
	N	Mean*	S.D.	N	Mean*	S.D.	N	Mean*	S.D.
February									
Boys	32	112·09	23·14	65	101·95	19·15	97	105·30	21·10
Girls	41	99·66	18·46	52	103·13	17·84	93	101·60	18·20
All	73	105·11	21·55	117	102·48	18·59	190	103·48	19·81
April									
Boys	61	108·69	19·39	55	104·93	21·40	116	106·91	20·45
Girls	43	105·86	23·26	68	99·49	20·72	111	101·95	21·96
All	104	107·51	21·13	123	101·92	20·20	227	104·48	21·45
June									
Boys	36	103·69	19·22	72	104·76	19·87	108	104·41	19·66
Girls	41	111·76	22·59	73	98·70	19·64	114	103·32	21·69
All	77	107·99	21·46	145	101·71	19·98	222	103·88	20·72
August									
Boys	40	106·08	16·89	68	98·34	18·56	108	101·20	18·35
Girls	38	100·42	17·91	75	99·72	21·02	113	99·96	20·04
All	78	103·32	17·62	143	99·06	19·93	221	100·57	19·24
October									
Boys	30	109·07	14·10	52	104·00	24·16	82	105·85	21·18
Girls	37	101·54	15·96	59	96·85	19·44	96	98·65	18·32
All	67	104·91	15·61	111	100·20	22·07	178	101·97	20·02
December									
Boys	28	98·32	17·02	56	104·57	18·23	84	102·49	18·08
Girls	44	100·39	17·58	49	96·30	18·47	93	98·24	18·17
All	72	99·58	17·37	105	100·71	18·80	177	100·25	18·25
TOTAL									
Boys	227	106·69	19·089	368	102·97	20·322	595	104·39	19·923
Girls	244	103·32	20·003	376	99·06	19·839	620	100·73	20·012
All	471	104·94	19·645	744	100·99	20·163	1,215	102·52	20·056

BINET THOUSAND (1932)—STANFORD REVISION

	Cities			Counties			Whole Country		
	N	Mean*	S.D.	N	Mean*	S.D.	N	Mean*	S.D.
Boys	189	105·93	16·72	311	100·80	16·53	500	102·74	17·34
Girls	194	101·59	16·24	306	99·28	15·90	500	100·71	16·63
All	383	103·73	16·74	617	100·05	16·63	1,000	101·46	16·77

* Calculated direct from individual IQs

Appendix I

Eighty-nine children from the four cities were given both the Stanford (1916) and the Terman-Merrill (1937) Revisions, sometimes simultaneously and sometimes successively in the order 1916 followed by 1937, or vice versa. Their individual scores in both tests are given below:

Boys (39)			Girls (50)		
	Terman-Merrill	Stanford		Terman-Merrill	Stanford
	IQ	IQ		IQ	IQ
S	160	157	A	146	145
S	157	140	S	134	119
S	137	139	S	133	129
S	136	142	S	129	116
S	130	129	A	127	117
A	126	117	S	126	126
S	122	118	S	124	118
S	119	117	A	122	118
S	116	122	S	116	124
S	116	105	S	113	112
S	112	102	S	113	105
S	111	104	A	113	102
S	111	102	B	112	101
S	111	102	S	111	98
S	109	117	S	108	93
S	109	99	S	105	105
A	106	97	A	105	90
A	104	111	S	104	101
S	104	96	S	104	101
A	103	98	S	101	91
A	102	110	A	101	88
A	99	100	S	96	89
A	99	92	A	94	87
A	99	92	A	94	86
S	96	92	B	94	91
A	95	93	A	93	96
A	93	86	A	93	92
A	92	97	A	93	89
S	91	82	A	93	97
B	86	88	A	92	94
A	86	83	A	90	90
A	83	84	A	87	84
B	81	83	S	86	88
S	81	79	A	84	87
S	79	79	A	83	84
A	78	88	S	82	87
A	75	77	S	82	82

Boys (*contd.*)			Girls (*contd.*)		
	Terman-Merill	*Stanford*		*Terman-Merill*	*Stanford*
S	72	68	A	81	89
S	66	63	B	81	77
			A	81	74
Mean	103·90	101·28	S	79	79
S.D.	21·32	20·61	S	79	79
			S	78	73
			A	78	85
			S	77	77
			A	75	76
			S	75	75
			S	73	78
			S	68	71
			S	65	71
			Mean	97·46	94·52
			S.D.	19·35	16·76

	All (89)	
	Terman-Merrill	*Stanford*
Mean	100·28	97·48
S.D.	20·36	18·85

		All	Boys	Girls
A	Terman-Merrill first, Stanford second	36	15	21
B	Stanford first, Terman-Merrill second	5	2	3
S	Simultaneously	48	22	26
	Total	89	39	50

It appears that for this group the 1937 Terman-Merrill L scale gives a mean IQ of 100·28, while the 1916 Stanford Revision mean for the same children is 97·48, with a significant difference in favour of the Terman-Merrill L scale of 2·80 points of IQ. The respective standard deviations are 20·36 on the Terman-Merrill Revision and 18·85 on the Stanford Revision, indicating the greater variability of the Terman-Merrill scores for this group. The correlation between the two sets of scores is $r = 0.95$, which indicates a high degree of agreement in the ranking of the pupils by the two scales. More detailed statistical treatment of these data is given in Chapter VIII.

APPENDIX II

TERMAN-MERRILL IQs OF NINETY-FIVE ABSENTEES FROM GROUP TEST

IQ	IQ	Percentiles	IQ	Percentiles	IQ
166	101	100	166		
156	101	90	129		
150	101			84	119
146	100	80	118		
144	98			75	116
139	97	70	113		
133	97	60	105		
131	97	50	102	Median	102
130	97	40	97		
129	93	30	88		
125	92			25	81
123	92	20	79		
123	91			16	77
122	90	10	74		
121	90	0	61		
120	89				
119	88				
118	88				
118	88				
117	84				
117	83				
117	83				
116	82				
116	81				
114	80				
113	80				
113	79				
113	79				
113	78				
111	78				
110	77				
108	77				
108	76				
107	76				
107	76				
105	75				
105	74				
105	74				
105	72				
105	70				
104	70				
103	69				
103	69				
103	68				
102	68				
102	65				
102	61				
102					

Semi-interquartile range
i.e. $\frac{1}{2}(116 - 81) = 17\cdot5$

$\frac{1}{2}(84\text{th} - 16\text{th percentile})$
i.e. $\frac{1}{2}(119 - 77) = 21\cdot0$

IQ	Frequency	
160-166	1 ⎫	
150-159	2 ⎬ 9	
140-149	2 ⎪	
130-139	4 ⎭	
120-129	7 ⎫ 22	
110-119	15 ⎭	
100-109	21 ⎫ 32	
90- 99	11 ⎭	
80- 89	11 ⎫ 26	
70- 79	15 ⎭	
60- 69	6	6

Mean 100·56
S.D. 21·89

APPENDIX III

TERMAN-MERRILL IQs AND VERBAL TEST SCORES OF SIX-DAY SAMPLE

Cities: Boys.   N = 227

February IQ	V*	April IQ	V	June IQ	V	August IQ	V	October IQ	V	December IQ	V
173	71	169	69	142	64	164	66	140	55	140	60
157	64	155	66	140	48	143	60	131	51	127	47
152	68	138	60	137	57	132	57	128	56	126	55
151	63	138	56	137	55	131	53	127	46	124	44
133	xx	134	60	133	61	130	52	125	61	123	55
130	58	133	65	127	57	122	51	123	52	109	35
126	52	131	47	120	46	122	49	123	45	106	43
126	49	130	64	118	43	118	47	121	xx	104	37
125	55	130	55	117	55	114	xx	117	44	103	37
120	60	128	55	117	39	113	41	117	40	102	xx
119	53	127	61	111	50	112	18	113	52	102	47
119	45	127	54	111	47	112	02	113	40	99	35
118	52	126	56	108	44	110	41	113	xx	99	26
113	45	125	55	105	49	109	56	112	41	98	31
111	46	125	54	105	44	107	47	110	28	97	04
109	57	124	47	103	xx	107	28	109	50	96	40
107	51	123	55	100	33	105	47	109	55	95	30
104	41	122	56	98	43	105	47	106	37	92	xx
104	22	122	xx	98	38	105	44	103	31	87	23
102	34	120	45	98	34	105	44	101	40	87	13
102	xx	118	48	98	34	104	49	100	31	86	26
101	48	116	60	98	30	103	26	98	35	86	15
100	33	116	54	98	27	102	57	98	27	83	10
98	28	115	52	97	34	101	27	94	43	78	20
96	36	112	47	96	36	101	xx	94	37	77	11
94	19	111	45	96	36	100	46	93	35	76	01
93	52	110	49	95	42	98	37	92	45	76	xx
87	18	108	53	93	15	98	14	90	32	75	16
86	25	107	46	92	xx	97	xx	88	xx		
79	26	107	38	92	16	93	24	84	01		
77	28	106	44	89	28	93	16				
75	03	104	30	79	08	92	32				
		104	30	77	15	91	31				
		102	57	72	xx	91	28				
		102	32	70	xx	90	34				
		102	42	66	00	89	31				
		101	46			87	29				
		100	39			87	22				
		99	35			81	12				
		99	06			79	12				
		98	36								
		98	24								
		97	30								
		97	26								
		95	38								
		93	37								
		93	34								
		92	37								

April (cont.)

IQ	V
90	34
90	29
90	xx
89	27
87	25
86	28
86	18
85	23
82	33
82	32
82	22
77	06
75	04

* xx denotes an absentee from the group test and yy a pupil unable to attempt it.

TERMAN-MERRILL IQs AND VERBAL TEST SCORES OF SIX-DAY SAMPLE

Cities: Girls. N = 244

February		April		June		August		October		December	
IQ	V	IQ	V	IQ	V	IQ	V	IQ	V	IQ	V
143	62	170	66	166	xx	142	60	148	61	146	xx
139	62	156	xx	158	65	139	62	131	61	133	55
135	68	146	64	156	70	136	59	131	50	131	46
127	57	140	58	152	52	133	51	128	52	127	51
125	63	138	59	140	71	121	50	123	59	125	40
121	36	138	57	140	63	117	55	123	xx	124	51
120	54	129	xx	133	60	115	55	115	53	122	48
119	58	128	61	133	54	115	53	111	48	119	66
117	58	121	61	130	xx	113	xx	111	42	117	52
112	52	121	44	126	51	111	38	110	39	113	43
112	51	120	57	123	53	108	51	107	44	110	52
110	55	120	44	121	54	107	44	107	40	109	49
110	51	118	50	120	49	103	42	106	30	109	36
107	46	116	56	118	58	102	49	105	51	108	43
107	46	113	41	115	57	101	38	104	37	107	41
105	45	111	54	114	50	99	40	103	33	106	42
104	47	111	xx	113	48	99	37	101	xx	106	40
101	38	108	51	113	47	99	35	100	40	106	36
100	47	105	44	113	xx	99	32	98	30	106	31
95	48	105	43	111	50	99	32	97	38	105	xx
95	37	104	47	111	32	98	35	93	27	103	37
93	42	102	37	109	45	97	23	92	41	97	32
93	40	100	53	108	42	97	xx	91	34	96	39
93	32	99	50	105	27	96	35	91	33	95	21
90	27	99	37	103	62	95	44	91	11	94	39
89	40	97	xx	103	38	95	28	91	09	94	24
88	36	96	48	101	41	93	39	91	xx	93	36
87	43	96	43	96	40	91	31	90	42	93	25
87	20	96	38	96	32	90	28	90	34	93	22
86	24	95	40	95	43	87	30	90	30	92	41
86	16	92	33	92	36	87	19	88	25	88	34
84	28	89	26	91	36	86	31	88	14	88	23
83	15	88	22	91	19	78	26	85	38	87	26
82	40	87	42	89	30	78	16	84	04	87	22
81	25	87	39	89	27	76	26	83	29	84	26
81	24	84	06	89	25	75	25	82	01	83	33
80	28	81	28	85	35	74	15	78	25	83	18
79	33	80	32	85	31	65	xx			81	30
78	29	80	23	79	18					81	21
74	18	78	28	74	xx					78	12
68	xx	75	26							78	xx
		75	25							77	27
		58	YY							75	20
										68	xx

TERMAN-MERRILL IQs AND VERBAL TEST SCORES OF SIX-DAY SAMPLE

Counties: Boys. N = 368

February		April		June		August		October		December	
IQ	V	IQ	V	IQ	V	IQ	V	IQ	V	IQ	V
148	61	162	64	150	xx	142	59	170	72	167	70
143	55	156	64	147	69	138	54	165	64	149	59
138	53	147	64	145	67	137	45	154	56	147	58
136	53	145	59	141	62	128	47	144	54	134	57
130	63	140	62	138	68	127	51	139	51	132	57
128	65	132	63	135	57	126	54	130	53	129	57
125	56	131	53	134	64	119	50	128	45	127	51
124	62	130	45	131	58	119	49	127	44	127	34
124	55	124	53	130	55	119	41	126	57	120	xx
120	28	123	61	129	55	118	55	125	53	116	49
119	53	120	57	125	49	118	44	124	51	114	33
118	62	120	39	123	45	118	25	123	56	113	44
118	53	119	54	123	xx	116	46	122	49	111	44
115	55	118	51	122	55	114	33	121	57	111	36
115	38	118	49	122	49	111	53	121	45	110	45
114	56	113	55	121	50	111	51	117	xx	110	40
113	xx	113	53	118	54	109	50	114	47	110	29
112	38	113	45	118	43	109	44	112	37	110	xx
112	37	112	39	118	xx	109	41	109	10	108	xx
111	52	111	62	117	xx	108	51	106	43	107	36
111	48	111	54	116	50	108	43	106	42	107	xx
110	22	109	41	116	xx	107	45	105	27	106	26
109	62	108	xx	116	xx	106	45	104	37	106	24
109	39	106	62	114	36	105	47	104	36	106	12
107	51	106	55	113	52	105	41	103	46	105	49
107	45	106	36	113	47	105	24	103	35	104	51
105	45	104	45	112	53	105	22	101	22	103	51
105	xx	104	42	112	47	104	40	100	45	102	38
104	46	103	38	112	36	103	44	96	34	102	26
104	45	103	34	111	48	103	28	95	43	102	24
104	36	103	xx	110	34	102	xx	95	32	101	49
103	46	101	17	108	29	101	47	94	27	101	35
102	36	100	48	108	28	101	26	93	32	100	47
102	34	98	27	106	42	100	29	93	30	100	09
101	47	98	08	105	xx	99	52	91	03	99	23
101	38	97	38	105	xx	99	05	90	xx	99	20
101	xx	97	24	103	30	96	44	88	43	99	08
100	44	91	40	102	44	96	25	88	20	98	54
100	40	91	39	102	33	96	04	86	12	98	xx
100	37	91	22	102	04	95	32	85	20	96	32
100	xx	88	26	99	42	95	30	85	11	96	15
99	45	86	24	98	36	94	29	84	16	95	05

TERMAN-MERRILL IQs AND VERBAL TEST SCORES OF SIX-DAY SAMPLE

Counties: Boys (continued).

February		April		June		August		October		December	
IQ	V	IQ	V	IQ	V	IQ	V	IQ	V	IQ	V
99	32	86	11	98	19	94	11	83	xx	93	27
99	25	85	21	98	06	93	29	80	28	93	10
97	xx	83	30	97	34	91	36	79	15	93	09
95	32	82	21	96	35	91	17	79	05	89	07
91	45	82	xx	96	28	90	29	74	11	87	08
91	33	81	04	95	33	90	15	74	11	85	20
89	xx	80	xx	94	46	88	14	73	32	85	12
87	23	79	14	94	43	88	13	71	06	85	11
87	17	78	05	92	35	87	34	70	xx	84	19
84	23	73	21	91	37	86	34	59	YY	83	21
82	37	73	17	91	19	82	33			80	27
82	27	71	02	89	13	82	26			77	18
82	27	70	08	89	07	81	38			77	02
81	22			88	33	80	xx			68	04
79	27			87	30	79	29				
78	03			87	22	75	21				
76	17			85	34	75	11				
72	16			84	24	72	12				
70	30			84	17	72	06				
70	04			83	xx	70	00				
68	12			81	28	69	00				
63	00			81	26	69	xx				
58	YY			81	00	68	06				
				79	28	66	28				
				78	27	65	09				
				77	33	63	YY				
				76	25						
				76	xx						
				65	00						
				61	xx						

Terman-Merrill IQs and Verbal Test Scores of Six-Day Sample

Counties: Girls.   N = 376

February		April		June		August		October		December	
IQ	V	IQ	V	IQ	V	IQ	V	IQ	V	IQ	V
146	65	151	70	151	64	162	70	144	xx	150	55
132	60	144	64	144	57	151	64	140	60	128	50
131	xx	142	64	142	53	144	60	133	54	127	59
130	63	139	xx	140	49	138	58	132	54	126	54
130	62	135	55	132	55	133	63	132	50	124	59
125	xx	134	62	132	55	131	42	125	53	119	37
124	56	131	56	124	59	128	57	124	50	118	46
122	57	129	56	124	52	128	57	122	52	116	48
122	46	128	47	123	58	128	11	122	50	113	48
120	55	121	51	123	41	124	59	120	56	112	56
119	62	121	43	122	56	122	50	119	50	111	34
119	50	120	55	119	xx	122	36	116	51	107	35
118	54	119	44	118	36	118	56	111	46	106	56
117	47	118	59	117	38	118	49	110	37	106	50
117	xx	118	55	115	53	118	43	109	30	105	43
116	46	116	37	115	44	118	36	108	37	103	33
115	49	114	49	115	31	118	xx	107	xx	103	26
113	63	111	50	114	54	115	53	106	22	102	49
112	52	110	46	111	43	115	45	105	xx	102	40
111	49	108	40	108	42	110	48	104	34	102	37
109	43	106	50	108	37	110	47	103	39	101	46
108	40	105	51	107	51	109	42	103	xx	101	27
105	49	104	49	107	44	109	39	102	46	98	16
104	55	104	43	107	42	108	41	102	44	97	54
104	44	103	46	105	40	107	40	102	xx	97	36
103	50	103	44	104	44	106	52	101	32	97	34
103	45	102	37	104	39	106	50	96	39	93	32
102	40	101	44	103	34	105	44	95	46	92	34
101	04	101	42	102	31	105	32	93	39	91	45
100	53	101	38	99	42	104	49	93	18	91	19
99	44	101	22	99	35	104	xx	92	34	90	29
97	51	99	52	99	31	100	45	92	34	90	25
96	37	98	41	98	37	100	33	91	15	89	46
96	33	96	44	97	41	99	41	88	39	85	28
94	37	96	34	96	43	99	33	88	22	85	18
93	46	96	07	96	37	99	28	87	32	80	17
88	35	95	42	95	47	98	41	86	28	79	13
88	xx	95	35	95	43	98	30	86	25	79	06
87	49	94	45	95	42	97	50	85	27	78	23
87	35	94	28	95	39	97	34	84	xx	78	xx
87	25	93	44	95	38	97	28	83	18	76	15
85	31	93	39	93	29	96	43	83	18	76	13

TERMAN-MERRILL IQs AND VERBAL TEST SCORES OF SIX-DAY SAMPLE

Counties: Girls (continued).

February		April		June		August		October		December	
IQ	V	IQ	V	IQ	V	IQ	V	IQ	V	IQ	V
83	36	93	35	92	30	96	30	83	15	76	12
83	33	93	XX	92	18	92	42	82	30	76	07
82	33	92	40	92	05	92	36	81	25	76	06
82	26	92	39	91	51	92	31	81	XX	68	10
79	41	90	38	90	34	91	31	80	03	68	00
78	31	89	50	89	08	91	23	78	35	67	04
78	25	88	43	88	27	90	27	78	25	65	00
78	15	87	44	88	25	90	26	77	27		
77	24	86	56	88	XX	90	24	76	16		
68	14	86	28	87	21	88	29	76	XX		
		85	33	85	18	88	02	74	05		
		82	34	84	35	87	27	74	XX		
		82	27	84	32	85	24	72	15		
		81	35	84	25	85	19	71	27		
		78	29	84	10	85	16	70	31		
		78	24	83	49	84	39	69	XX		
		77	XX	83	25	84	25	68	05		
		75	11	82	29	84	20				
		72	14	79	31	81	23				
		71	12	79	18	80	23				
		71	09	79	12	79	25				
		70	12	78	33	79	XX				
		70	10	78	30	79	XX				
		65	03	77	XX	78	21				
		62	18	75	23	78	08				
		61	18	72	17	75	07				
				72	16	75	XX				
				70	23	73	20				
				69	30	67	16				
				63	04	66	30				
				60	29	66	04				
						63	19				
						52	YY				

V

CORRECTION OF SCRIPTS AND CODING OF SOCIOLOGICAL SCHEDULES

WHEN the 1932 mental survey was contemplated it was intended that the correction of the scripts should be undertaken by a body of workers acting under the expert direction of the Research Council, but the magnitude of the task rendered this impossible, and in the end the scripts for the largest areas were corrected by the teachers, the schools being closed for this purpose on the afternoon of the day on which the test was applied.[1]

The 1947 survey was undertaken on the understanding that teachers should not be expected to correct the scripts. The General Secretary of the Educational Institute of Scotland thereupon assumed responsibility for the correction, intending to enlist teams of voluntary workers for this purpose. The task again proved too formidable for this procedure to be adopted, and resort had to be made to the Training Colleges, local committees of teachers, and small teams of voluntary workers to overtake the work.

The Training Colleges were approached in the following terms:

The Director of Studies

As you are aware, the Research Council is undertaking another mental survey in June of this year, and to accelerate the marking of the scripts it has been suggested that the students of the six Training Colleges might be enlisted to assist, each College to undertake the assessment of the scripts

---

[1] cf. *The Intelligence of Scottish Children*, p. 13.

of its own city. As the results of this survey will doubtless be constantly cited during the professional life of the students, it was thought that these would have more significance to them if the students felt they had personally participated in the survey.

I need not say how grateful the Research Council would be if your College could undertake this project.

The response was such that practically half the scripts were corrected by the end of June. The Research Council trusts that the benefit derived by the students from marking and checking the scripts was as great as it was to the Council.

Teams of voluntary workers were enlisted by the directors of education of Ayrshire, Clackmannan, East Lothian, Fife, Kirkcudbright, and Perth and Kinross, and by local branches of the Educational Institute in Dundee, Glasgow, Bute, Clackmannan, Dumfriesshire, Orkney, Renfrewshire and Zetland.

Special acknowledgment must be made of the team of ex-teachers who from September 1947 to March 1948 met twice a week at 46 Moray Place, Edinburgh, and corrected and checked over 7000 tests at an average rate of 125 per hour.

CORRECTION AND CHECKING OF SCRIPTS
MARKING ARRANGEMENTS

As one of the purposes of the 1947 mental survey was the comparison of the intelligence of Scottish children born in 1936 (1947 survey) with that of the pupils born in 1921 (1932 survey), the marking of the 1947 survey scripts was made to conform as closely as possible to that of the 1932 survey.[1]

The marking key for pages 3-8 of the test was the same as that used in 1932, each page being set out separately on strips of stout paper with the answers spaced to correspond with the spacing of the questions in the test. Page 2 was not marked.

[1] *The Intelligence of Scottish Children*, pp. 143-6.

A few days after the tests had been given, a group of about 130 students of Moray House Training College began both the marking and coding of the Edinburgh scripts and schedules as a " pilot " survey to find the most economical methods of marking and coding. The procedure finally adopted as most efficient formed the basis for the instructions to other marking groups. These instructions appear in detail in Appendices I, II and III, pp. 75-8.

The test scripts and the sociological schedules arrived in separate bundles from each school, and the first step was to pair off each script with its appropriate schedule. Each pupil within the school was given a serial number, beginning with 1 in each school. By this means, reference to the school's official number and the pupil's serial number made it possible to identify any individual script or schedule. A similar scheme was used for private or independent schools.

The scripts and schedules were then passed to a team of markers and checkers, and the test scores for P (picture test, p. 3) and V (verbal test, pp. 4-8) were entered in the schedules. The entry for pupils who were absent from the test was X, and the entry Y was used for those pupils who, for reasons of physical or mental defect, were unable to do the test. Further reference to the test scripts could now be dispensed with, and future operations conducted with the schedules alone.

PRACTICAL OBSERVATIONS

As the marking and checking of some 71,000 scripts entailed a very considerable amount of time and labour, the following observations may be of interest to those likely to be engaged on similar tasks.

It was found that it was essential to have the marking checked. On the first check a small, but not negligible amount of error (mainly omitted items and wrong addition) was found and rectified. A number of scripts were subjected to a second check, and though a few errors were still found, these were sufficiently small and infrequent to have no effect on the final findings of the survey.

Marking by teams was found to be the most economical method. A team of 14 could manage comfortably at least 120 scripts marked, checked and entered per hour, though the initial rate for the first hour or more was somewhat slower. Such a team of 14 persons was faster than two "half-teams" of 8 persons, and two "half-teams" were in turn faster than 14 individuals working independently, who could mark, check and enter an aggregate of approximately 100 tests per hour. A team of 14, however, required considerable floor and table space, and for this reason marking by smaller teams often proved more suitable in practice.

COMPARISON WITH 1932 SURVEY

The circumstances under which the scripts for both surveys were marked were very similar. Both used the same marking key and in both the marking was done by a number of groups working in different centres. As the test used was not wholly objective a certain number of discrepancies in the interpretation of doubtful answers was bound to arise. Samples of about 1000 tests each, drawn from the different marking groups, were taken from both surveys. Comparison of these two samples showed (a) that the actual amount of discrepancy was extremely small, (b) that most of the discrepancies appeared to be in scripts where scores were around the average, and (c) that the discrepancies were of the same nature and frequency in both surveys.

In view of the fact that the same procedure of marking and checking was used in both the 1947 and 1932 surveys and that inspection of the corrected scripts showed a degree of error so small as to be negligible, it can be concluded that any comparisons or measures made from the test results will not be vitiated to any significant extent by marking error.

CODING THE SOCIOLOGICAL SCHEDULES

For each pupil in the survey age group, as indicated in Chapter II, there was completed a sociological schedule, and for each pupil in the thirty-six-day-sample group and for each twin there was also a random-sample sociological schedule. It then became necessary to convert the information given in these schedules into a system of code numbers, so that these numbers could be punched on cards for use with the Hollerith counter-sorter machine.

In June 1947 the schedules of the Edinburgh schools were coded at Moray House by a group of students. During the following year about one thousand random-sample schedules were coded by the Survey Committee's office staff, and Professor Glass supervised the coding of the " Occupation of parent or guardian " in all the random-sample schedules in accordance with the classification used by the Royal Commission on Population. By June 1948 all schedules had been received, and the Edinburgh Provincial Committee and the Director of Studies agreed to suspend the Moray House Training College classes for three days to enable the remainder of the schedules to be coded. The three days proved adequate for the coding of some 8000 random-sample and 75,000 ordinary schedules. Thanks are due to those members of the Moray House staff, to the students, and to the retired teachers who assisted in this task. Particular mention should be made of the group of ex-Service men students who assisted in both 1947 and 1948.

On the basis of the experience gained in June 1947 sets of coding instructions were prepared. For some items these had to be given in considerable detail, as the information available was not always susceptible of clear-cut classification. These detailed instructions will appear in subsequent reports on the aspects of the sociological data to which they refer. The general coding instructions, however, are given in Appendix III, p. 78.

The coding was done by teams of students, and each schedule was both coded and checked. The majority of the schedules were checked once again, and a sample of over 2,500 schedules showed an error of less than 0·1%.

The coded schedules were then despatched to the Glasgow office of the British Tabulating Machine Company, where the cards were punched; and the sociological data were subsequently sorted and classified on the Hollerith counter-sorter at Moray House.

Appendix I

MARKING ARRANGEMENTS

1. The marking of tests is most quickly done by teams of 14 persons, each person marking or checking one page. It is recommended that one be solely engaged in marking the first page, another solely on the second, and so on.

2. The best division of labour within each team is as follows:

Nos. 1 and 2   Mark and check page 3 (the picture test)
Nos. 3 and 4   „   „   „   „ 4
Nos. 5 and 6   „   „   „   „ 5
Nos. 7 and 8   „   „   „   „ 6
Nos. 9 and 10   „   „   „   „ 7
Nos. 11 and 12   „   „   „   „ 8
Nos. 13 and 14   Check the addition, enter the scores in boxes P and V, and the serial number, on the schedule, and check that the serial number on test and schedule correspond.

3. A team of 8 persons is also satisfactory. If the half-team of 8 is being used, each pair should mark and check two pages of the test before passing it on to the next pair. The last pair, Nos. 7 and 8, should still check the addition and enter the scores and serial number on the schedules.

4. If a single person is marking a set of tests, it is recommended that he correct the first page of the tests, then return and correct the second page of the tests, and so on. The marking key is thereby more easily memorised.

5. The schedules should accompany each batch of tests being marked. Tests and schedules should be arranged in the same order and serially numbered within the school, i.e. for each school the numbering should start afresh at 1. Teachers were requested to arrange the tests and schedules in alphabetical order, boys first and then girls, but this may not have been done in all cases.

Appendix II

MARKING INSTRUCTIONS

1. Each marker and checker will receive a copy of the answer key and notes for correction. These must be strictly followed, even if occasionally a case arises where some other answer appears plausible. The only permissible answers are those given in the marking key and in the notes for correction.[1] The answer must be complete, and in full agreement with the marking key before it is marked correct. If more than one answer is given, it is wrong; if the pupil's answer is not clear, it is wrong. Only when the pupil gives the correct answer clearly (and no other answer), but in a form other than that required by the test, is the answer marked correct, e.g. the pupil writes the correct word instead of underlining it.

2. Tests are best marked with a coloured pencil. Each item correct should be marked in the right hand margin with a long dash (——). This is better than a tick (√). No mark should be made against incorrect or omitted answers.

The marker's mark in red pencil is put opposite each correct answer. The total of the correct answers is then entered at the foot of the page and in the appropriate space on the front page of the test. The test is then passed on to the checker.

3. When the marking is being checked, it is recommended that the check consist of a complete re-marking of the test in differently coloured pencil. Dashes should be entered as shown (——), the checker's dash projecting beyond that of the original marker's. Page and total addition should be checked throughout. Agreement of the two sets of marks, i.e. checker's and marker's, does not ensure that the addition is necessarily correct. Checkers should aim at ignoring the marker's marks, and be on the alert for correct answers unmarked by the marker.

The correct items should again be added, the total being entered at the foot of the page, and the total on the front page initialled as correct. The test is then passed on to the next marker, open at the next unmarked page.

[1] *The Intelligence of Scottish Children*, pp. 143-6.

4. It is recommended that the scores should be entered in the sociological schedules immediately the marking is completed. For this purpose the schedules will be issued with each batch of tests, and it is important that the order should be kept the same for schedules and tests. If a team of markers and checkers is engaged, one member should be allocated to the duty of checking the addition on the front page and of entering the scores in the schedule. The serial number should also be checked and entered at the foot of the schedule. The total score for the picture test (p. 3) is entered in the box marked P on the sociological schedule, and the total for the rest of the test in the box marked V. *See that the schedule is for the same pupil as the test.*

If the score in the verbal test is, for example, 65, enter 6 in the first box and 5 in the second, but if the score is less than 10, enter 0 in the first box and the unit in the second, e.g. a score of 5 is entered as 05.

If there is a sociological schedule but no test, the assumption is that the pupil was absent. The entry in boxes P and V of the schedule should be X, XX. In the case of a mentally or physically handicapped child who has not attempted the test, the entry should be Y, YY.

The serial number should be entered on the schedule on the same principle, e.g. 001, 010, 100.

APPENDIX III

GENERAL CODING INSTRUCTIONS

1. The process of coding consists of converting the information given in the sociological schedules into a system of numbers, e.g. " Boy " may be coded as 1, " Girl " as 2. These numbers are subsequently punched on cards, so that they may be counted and sorted by machine.

2. These code numbers are to be *clearly* entered in the boxes in the right-hand margin of the schedules. The boxes are not always exactly opposite the question asked, so it is important to see that the code number is entered in the correct box. Ink is better than pencil.

Detailed instructions are issued on separate sheets, but the following rules apply:

(*a*) All boxes must be filled, e.g. if there are three boxes and the code number is 7, the entry is 007; or if the code number is 30, the entry is 030.

(*b*) " Direct entry " means that the number given as the answer is entered in the box, e.g. " Official number of school " is given as 103; the entry is 0103.

(*c*) If the answer is not given in the schedule and cannot be worked out from other answers, code number is X. X means " Information not available ".

N.B. This does not apply to Item 9 (*Date of birth*).

4. The schedules have been divided into five sections and a separate coding instruction issued for each section. Coders, therefore, should work in groups of ten, one pair coding and checking for each section. The first of each pair should code the answer, and the second check by translating the code number back into the original answer and checking that it is correct. (For random-sample schedules, which will be coded separately, there are seven sections, and teams will therefore consist of fourteen members.)

5. These separate coding instructions give detailed directions as to code numbers to be used. *Read them very carefully and follow them exactly.*

VI

RESULTS OF GROUP TEST

In the 1932 Scottish mental survey the attempt was made
to test a complete year group of Scottish pupils, those
born in 1921. This group included mentally defective
children and such types of the physically defective as
could reasonably be expected to attempt the test.[1] Test
scores were therefore available for almost all born in
1921 who were attending school on 1st June 1932, and
from these scores were compiled the tables of results
which appear in *The Intelligence of Scottish Children.*

NUMBERS TESTED IN 1947

In the 1947 survey the net was more widely cast. The
schools were requested to complete a sociological schedule (see Appendix I, pp. 36-7) for each pupil on the
roll at the date of the test, 4th June 1947, whether
the pupil was actually present to take the test on that
day or not. The test scores of the absentee pupils were
recorded as X, XX. The sociological schedule was also
completed for pupils who, in the opinion of the school
authorities, were unable to do the test by reason of
physical or mental defect. The test scores of such were
recorded as Y, YY.

In all, schedules were completed for 75,451 pupils.
The procedure by which the information contained in
these schedules was coded and transferred to punched
cards for classification by the Hollerith counter-sorter has

[1] *The Intelligence of Scottish Children*, pp. 22-3.

already been described. Before tables of results comparable with those of the 1932 survey could be constructed, however, it was found that the data for a certain number of pupils had to be discarded as incomplete in some respect. The sex of 16 and the month of birth of 21 had not been recorded. The verbal test scores of 24 were clearly in error (e.g. test scores of 81 out of a possible of 76), and the scores of a further 165 had not been recorded. The majority of this latter group can be accounted for by some two or three schools where the internal evidence from the test scripts clearly suggested that the test had not been administered in a proper manner. The test scores of such cases were not included. Finally, during the process of sorting, 14 cards were damaged, some irreparably. When the above cases are deducted from the total of 75,451, we are left with 75,211 pupils whose sex, month of birth and verbal test scores are known. Though it is possible that the errors and omissions of some of the 240 discarded cases listed above might have been discovered and rectified, this would have involved considerable time and labour, with the result that the publication of this report would have been unduly delayed. For the same reason, the scores on the picture test (pp. 2-3 of the test) have not been included in the present report.

Two further points require mention. Of the 75,211 pupils, 4,406, or 5·86%, were absent on the day of the test;[1] their scores appear as XX in the tables of test

[1] For comparison with the 1932 survey the following data are given:

	(i)	(ii)*	(iii)	(iii) as	(iii) as
	Registrar-	Scottish Education Department's	Number	%age of	%age of
Date of	General's	Official Number	taking	(i)	(ii)
Survey	Estimate	on Registers	Test		
1947	80,300	76,330	70,805	88·17	92·76
1932	100,300	96,028	87,498	87·23	91·12

* The Department's figures refer to a slightly different calendar year and apply only to pupils on the registers of grant-aided schools.

scores that follow. The 294 boys and 238 girls with scores recorded as YY, however, presented a minor problem, as they constitute a category which did not appear in the 1932 survey results. Such evidence as there is leads to the conclusion that they constitute a group of somewhat lower intelligence than those in 1932 who attempted to do the test and obtained a score of zero.[1]

It was decided, however, for the purposes of comparison to amalgamate the YY scores with the zero scores, and, unless otherwise stated, the score group 0-9 includes the YY scores. In all other respects the tables of the 1947 survey data presented below are directly comparable with the corresponding tables for the 1932 survey, and the calculations made on the two sets of results follow exactly the same procedures.

GROUP-TEST SCORES

Table IV gives the verbal test scores for 70,805 pupils born in each month throughout 1936. Table V gives the same data for the 87,498 born in 1921 who were tested in the 1932 survey. Tables VI and VII give the same data for boys only, and Tables VIII and IX for girls only.

[1] A sample of 289 scoring 0-9 inclusive in the verbal test was taken from the 1932 survey. Of these, 38, or 13·1%, scored zero. A sample of 231 with scores of 0-9 and YY, and from the same area, was taken from the 1947 survey. Of these, 7·8% scored zero and 34·2% had scores of YY. As the number scoring YY is exceptionally high in this area, the corresponding figures for the whole 1947 survey probably give a safer basis for comparison. Of the 5,091 scoring 0-9 and YY, 710, or 13·9%, scored zero, and 532, or 10·5%, scored YY. Further, of those who were individually tested, the 8 who scored zero on the verbal test have a mean IQ of 68, and the 5 who scored YY have a mean IQ of 58. It would appear that the 1947 survey had dredged more deeply into the lower levels of intelligence.

DISTRIBUTION OF VERBAL TEST SCORE BY MONTH OF BIRTH
Maximum 76 points

TABLE IV

Boys and Girls born in 1936

	0-9	10-19	20-29	30-39	40-49	50-59	60-69	70-76	Total	xx	Total
Jan.	335	405	712	1142	1589	1271	487	30	5971	329	6300
Feb.	299	393	659	1186	1475	1114	529	26	5681	342	6023
March	348	481	796	1370	1683	1311	496	20	6505	399	6904
April	381	501	823	1321	1653	1239	471	26	6415	357	6772
May	413	550	888	1372	1608	1102	418	16	6367	421	6788
June	466	547	824	1307	1585	1037	359	16	6141	403	6544
July	427	568	805	1276	1466	993	269	19	5823	342	6165
Aug.	434	552	897	1294	1353	913	253	18	5714	368	6082
Sept.	438	577	868	1246	1312	818	226	9	5494	347	5841
Oct.	464	649	900	1280	1325	781	206	10	5615	378	5993
Nov.	529	667	910	1216	1225	732	195	6	5480	336	5816
Dec.	557	699	996	1289	1261	636	156	5	5599	384	5983
	5091	6589	10078	15299	17535	11947	4065	201	70805	4406	75211

TABLE V

Boys and Girls born in 1921

	0-9	10-19	20-29	30-39	40-49	50-59	60-69	70-76	Total
Jan.	326	611	979	1596	1790	1328	401	17	7048
Feb.	374	588	959	1491	1653	1145	378	16	6604
March	414	681	1200	1720	1923	1226	354	25	7543
April	492	779	1199	1864	1987	1265	369	9	7964
May	529	857	1321	1914	1979	1169	334	11	8114
June	544	829	1231	1835	1751	1070	267	15	7542
July	535	851	1274	1784	1648	877	228	8	7205
Aug.	517	887	1321	1767	1680	843	187	9	7211
Sept.	554	920	1372	1753	1549	761	190	3	7102
Oct.	623	935	1264	1682	1564	695	159	6	6928
Nov.	637	975	1276	1656	1381	632	163	10	6730
Dec.	778	1189	1487	1827	1441	635	146	4	7507
	6323	10102	14883	20889	20346	11646	3176	133	87498

DISTRIBUTION OF VERBAL TEST SCORE BY MONTH OF BIRTH

TABLE VI

BOYS BORN IN 1936

	0-9	10-19	20-29	30-39	40-49	50-59	60-69	70-76	Total	xx	Total
Jan.	212	221	373	569	754	642	239	18	3028	158	3186
Feb.	202	238	326	579	710	548	264	9	2876	166	3042
March	214	252	411	680	828	661	255	12	3313	201	3514
April	251	256	438	645	793	616	250	13	3262	193	3455
May	265	303	449	687	748	534	211	12	3209	213	3422
June	282	287	408	654	737	507	178	8	3061	219	3280
July	264	286	401	627	702	470	146	10	2906	165	3071
Aug.	283	315	450	601	654	450	116	11	2880	191	3071
Sept.	266	326	438	622	644	416	126	6	2844	156	3000
Oct.	273	350	438	659	629	396	109	6	2860	176	3036
Nov.	325	361	479	574	551	370	93	3	2756	167	2923
Dec.	354	387	495	596	600	309	70	3	2814	184	2998
	3191	3582	5106	7493	8350	5919	2057	111	35809	2189	37998

TABLE VII

BOYS BORN IN 1921

	0-9	10-19	20-29	30-39	40-49	50-59	60-69	70-76	Total
Jan.	180	317	478	755	881	700	230	10	3551
Feb.	219	295	439	737	798	600	217	10	3315
March	240	331	582	830	957	635	187	13	3775
April	288	409	580	884	1008	660	205	7	4041
May	300	439	669	940	985	620	188	7	4148
June	308	417	599	909	851	571	152	10	3817
July	305	417	622	870	824	506	141	3	3688
Aug.	264	435	667	824	829	438	109	5	3571
Sept.	327	473	660	857	792	419	102	2	3632
Oct.	338	487	603	825	754	380	87	4	3478
Nov.	358	480	647	824	660	329	94	7	3399
Dec.	441	604	717	868	725	349	88	3	3795
	3568	5104	7263	10123	10064	6207	1800	81	44210

DISTRIBUTION OF VERBAL TEST SCORE BY MONTH OF BIRTH

TABLE VIII

GIRLS BORN IN 1936

	0-9	10-19	20-29	30-39	40-49	50-59	60-69	70-76	Total	xx	Total
Jan.	123	184	339	573	835	629	248	12	2943	171	3114
Feb.	97	155	333	607	765	566	265	17	2805	176	2981
March	134	229	385	690	855	650	241	8	3192	198	3390
April	130	245	385	676	860	623	221	13	3153	164	3317
May	148	247	439	685	860	568	207	4	3158	208	3366
June	184	260	416	653	848	530	181	8	3080	184	3264
July	163	282	404	649	764	523	123	9	2917	177	3094
Aug.	151	237	447	693	699	463	137	7	2834	177	3011
Sept.	172	251	430	624	668	402	100	3	2650	191	2841
Oct.	191	299	462	621	696	385	97	4	2755	202	2957
Nov.	204	306	431	642	674	362	102	3	2724	169	2893
Dec.	203	312	501	693	661	327	86	2	2785	200	2985
	1900	3007	4972	7806	9185	6028	2008	90	34996	2217	37213

TABLE IX

GIRLS BORN IN 1921

	0-9	10-19	20-29	30-39	40-49	50-59	60-69	70-76	Total
Jan.	146	294	501	841	909	628	171	7	3497
Feb.	155	293	520	754	855	545	161	6	3289
March	174	350	618	890	966	591	167	12	3768
April	204	370	619	980	979	605	164	2	3923
May	229	418	652	974	994	549	146	4	3966
June	236	412	632	926	900	499	115	5	3725
July	230	434	652	914	824	371	87	5	3517
Aug.	253	452	654	943	851	405	78	4	3640
Sept.	227	447	712	896	757	342	88	1	3470
Oct.	285	448	661	857	810	315	72	2	3450
Nov.	279	495	629	832	721	303	69	3	3331
Dec.	337	585	770	959	716	286	58	1	3712
	2755	4998	7620	10766	10282	5439	1376	52	43288

Disregarding for the present differences in age, and not taking the absentees into account, we obtain comparative measures of the test scores in the 1947 and 1932 surveys. These are given below in Table X.

TABLE X

MEANS, STANDARD DEVIATIONS AND MEDIAN SCORES
OF 1947 AND 1932 SURVEYS

Date of Survey	Sex	No. of Cases	Mean	S.D.	Median
1947	Both	70,805	36·741	16·102	38·42
1932		87,498	34·457	15·481	35·46
1947	Boys	35,809	35·880	16·68	37·54
1932		44,210	34·503	15·92	35·60
1947	Girls	34,996	37·622	15·44	39·26
1932		43,288	34·409	15·02	35·32

Examination of Table X reveals several points of interest. First is the fact that the mean score of all the 1947 pupils has increased by 2·284 points of score over the corresponding value for the 1932 survey. A very rough estimate would give this increase as equivalent to about two points of IQ. Secondly, though the average scores of both boys and girls are higher for 1947 than for 1932, the major proportion of the increase has been contributed by the girls, who have converted what was a very slight inferiority in 1932 into a significant superiority over the boys in 1947. The mean score of the 1947 boys exceeds that of the 1932 boys by 1·377 points, while the mean score of the 1947 girls is higher than that of the 1932 girls by 3·213 points of score. Finally, the standard deviation, which is a measure of the spread, or degree of dispersion, of the scores of the group tested, also shows an increase over the 1932 value. This increase, however, is mainly due to the boys, among whom there was in 1932 a greater range or scatter of intelligence than among the girls; in 1947 this feature is still present, but in a more marked degree. This difference between the spread of

H

ability between boys and girls can be further illustrated by the fact that, even though the girls' average score is higher, there are still 2·1% of the boys scoring 65 marks or more in the test, as compared with 1·8% of the girls.

A comparison of the distributions of the test scores for the 1947 and 1932 surveys is given in graphical form in Fig. 1, where the 1932 frequencies have been proportionately adjusted to make them comparable with the 1947 data, the total number of cases therefore becoming 70,805 for both distributions.

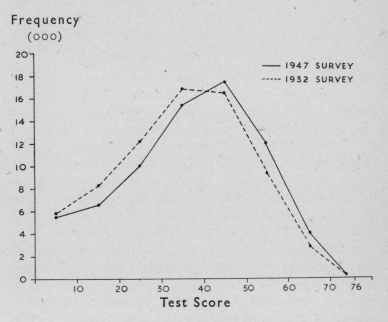

FIG. 1. DISTRIBUTION OF VERBAL TEST SCORES FOR ALL PUPILS: 1947 AND 1932 SURVEYS

Fig. 2 shows the distribution of test scores of the 1947 boys and girls separately, without adjustment of frequencies.

In these two graphs, the features which we have observed above are perhaps more clearly demonstrated. A

Frequency
(000)

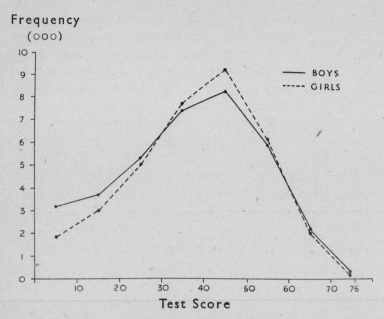

Test Score

FIG. 2. DISTRIBUTION OF VERBAL TEST SCORES FOR BOYS AND GIRLS (1947)

discussion of the possible reasons for, and implications of, these differences is reserved for later consideration; but it should be mentioned here that the differences between the 1947 and 1932 results, and between the 1947 boys and girls, as shown in Table X, are all statistically significant, and the probability of their being chance differences is almost infinitesimal. The difference between the 1947 and 1932 means for all, for example, is over 28 times its standard error, and the least difference, that between 1947 and 1932 girls' standard deviations, is 4·3 times its standard error.

So far we have been comparing the results from the two surveys without taking into account the ages of the pupils. It is well known, however, that the average scores in such intelligence tests increase with age, and an age difference of even one month will show an appreciable difference of score. In *The Intelligence of Scottish Children* (pp. 69-70) tables are presented giving the scores obtained at monthly intervals of age, at various levels of ability. It has not been considered necessary to repeat these calculations in full for the 1947 survey, only the 90, 84, 50 (median), 16 and 10 percentile levels being calculated on this occasion. Table XI presents the data for the boys, and Table XII for the girls. In Table XIII the data for boys and girls are combined, and in Table XIV are given the corresponding figures for the 84, 50 and 16 percentiles from the 1932 survey. Throughout, ages have been calculated to the nearest half month.

TABLE XI

Boys born in 1936

Born in	Age on Day of Test in Months	Percentiles				
		10	16	50	84	90
January	136½	13·16	20·88	41·34	55·96	58·79
February	135½	13·10	20·12	40·81	56·08	59·23
March	134½	14·15	21·06	40·70	55·52	58·53
April	133½	12·44	19·84	40·02	55·30	58·47
May	132½	11·34	17·70	38·05	54·06	57·67
June	131½	10·34	16·74	37·96	53·51	57·13
July	130½	10·43	16·53	37·51	52·93	56·64
August	129½	9·66	15·14	36·02	52·08	55·92
September	128½	10·06	15·30	35·80	51·73	55·84
October	127½	9·87	14·77	35·10	50·85	55·18
November	126½	7·98	12·71	33·21	50·18	54·65
December	125½	7·45	11·99	32·37	48·36	52·76

TABLE XII
Girls born in 1936

Born in	Age on Day of Test in Months	Percentiles				
		10	16	50	84	90
January	136½	18·81	24·33	42·52	56·15	58·95
February	135½	20·36	25·41	42·25	56·55	59·56
March	134½	17·59	23·34	41·35	55·47	58·42
April	133½	17·06	22·86	41·13	55·16	58·20
May	132½	16·29	22·01	40·20	54·32	57·65
June	131½	14·27	20·67	39·82	53·77	57·26
July	130½	14·06	20·04	38·89	53·10	56·45
August	129½	15·09	20·96	37·90	52·82	56·49
September	128½	13·21	19·52	37·06	51·51	55·47
October	127½	12·53	17·85	36·35	50·67	54·97
November	126½	11·74	17·08	36·06	50·36	54·88
December	125½	11·92	17·28	34·93	49·04	53·67

TABLE XIII
Boys and Girls born in 1936

Born in	Age on Day of Test in Months	Percentiles				
		10	16	50	84	90
January	136½	15·97	22·52	41·96	56·05	58·87
February	135½	16·35	22·79	41·56	56·32	59·38
March	134½	15·79	22·16	41·03	55·50	58·47
April	133½	14·70	21·25	40·60	55·23	58·33
May	132½	13·57	20·13	39·21	54·19	57·66
June	131½	12·21	18·94	38·94	53·64	57·19
July	130½	12·23	18·39	38·21	53·02	56·54
August	129½	11·99	18·20	37·03	52·45	56·21
September	128½	11·43	17·14	36·43	51·63	55·66
October	127½	11·00	16·19	35·71	50·76	55·08
November	126½	9·78	14·71	34·71	50·27	54·76
December	125½	9·54	14·35	33·75	48·72	53·23

TABLE XIV

BOYS AND GIRLS BORN IN 1921

Born in	Age on Day of Test in Months	Percentiles		
		16	50	84
January	136½	21·45	39·57	54·16
February	135½	20·49	38·76	53·71
March	134½	20·43	38·08	52·75
April	133½	19·53	37·61	52·41
May	132½	18·48	36·56	51·35
June	131½	17·49	35·86	50·86
July	130½	16·76	34·78	49·26
August	129½	16·68	34·48	48·82
September	128½	15·83	33·52	48·32
October	127½	14·69	33·32	47·91
November	126½	14·01	32·38	47·53
December	125½	13·06	31·14	46·61

From these tables the regression equations were found for each of the percentile ranks (P.R.) given above. The method used was that described in *The Intelligence of Scottish Children* (Appendix VII, p. 153). The regression equation is that of the " best fitting " straight line for each of the twelve monthly values at each of the percentile levels. The equations for these lines are given below. The small differences in the number of children born in the different months have been ignored, as these have no significant effect on the final values.

P.R.		All	Boys	Girls
90	1947	$S = ·510a - 10·022$	$S = ·525a - 11·991$	$S = ·498a - 8·405$
	1932		$S = ·61a - 25·0$	$S = ·67a - 34·1$
84	1947	$S = ·672a - 34·930$	$S = ·678a - 35·792$	$S = ·668a - 34·303$
	1932	$S = ·708a - 42·396$	$S = ·725a - 44·13$	$S = ·680a - 39·36$
50	1947	$S = ·761a - 61·380$	$S = ·819a - 69·840$	$S = ·708a - 53·753$
	1932	$S = ·739a - 61·349$	$S = ·786a - 67·38$	$S = ·693a - 55·47$
16	1947	$S = ·809a - 87·140$	$S = ·837a - 92·729$	$S = ·740a - 75·994$
	1932	$S = ·754a - 81·362$	$S = ·764a - 83·31$	$S = ·730a - 77·58$
10	1947	$S = ·646a - 71·695$	$S = ·562a - 62·789$	$S = ·746a - 82·548$
	1932		$S = ·55a - 60·6$	$S = ·57a - 61·7$

In these equations the coefficient of a (age in months) is the age allowance per month; thus boys born in January will, at the 50 percentile level or median, score on the average 0·819 points more than the boys born in February, who are a month younger; or, to put the same statement in another form, the score for boys of about average intelligence will increase by 0·819 points per month of age. It will be noted that the age allowance is not uniform for all levels of ability; it is least at the extremes and greatest in the region of the 16 percentile.

Figure 3 shows the regression lines derived from these equations for the 1947 boys and the 1947 girls respectively.

It is interesting to note that the superiority of the girls is most marked in the lower levels of score, the 90 and 84 percentiles for boys and girls lying so close together that it is not possible to represent them separately on this scale. The higher average score of the girls, therefore, does not denote a uniform superiority of the girls over the boys; it is rather the result of there being relatively fewer girls in the low-scoring groups. As previously pointed out, there are proportionately more boys than girls in the group making the highest scores in the test; but, on the other hand, the poorest 10% of the girls reach a score of about 15 as their upper limit, whereas the poorest 10% of the boys only reach a score of 10 points as their upper limit. There are, in fact, somewhat more very bright boys than very bright girls, but considerably more dull boys than dull girls. The greater spread of ability among the boys is again evident.

Figure 4, similarly, shows the regression lines for all in 1947 and 1932.

The values for the 1932 survey were taken from *The Intelligence of Scottish Children* (p. 64), where the equations for the 84, 50 and 16 percentiles are given. It will be observed that there is comparatively little difference

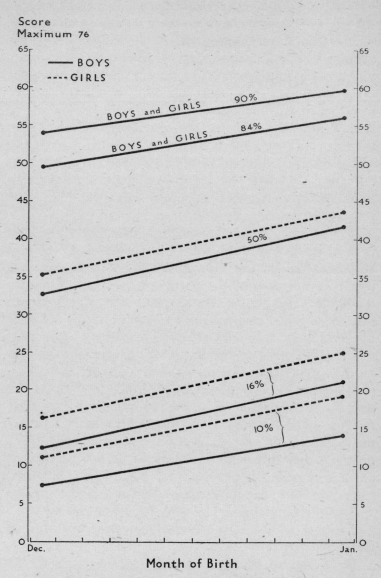

FIG. 3. REGRESSION LINES FOR BOYS AND GIRLS BORN IN 1936
(Test score on age by months)

Score
Maximum 76

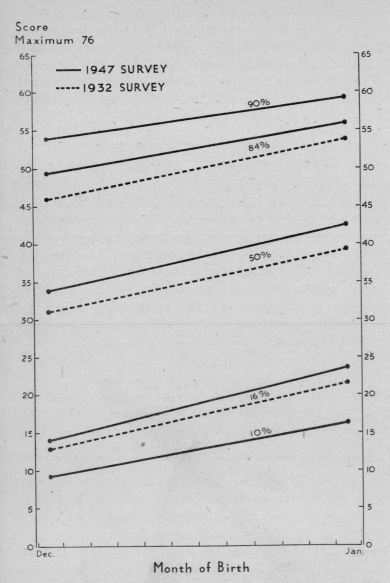

FIG. 4. REGRESSION LINES FOR 1947 AND 1932 (ALL PUPILS)
(Test score on age by months)

between the two surveys in the rate of increase of score with age. As would be expected from the results previously given, the values for 1947 are consistently higher than the corresponding 1932 values. The increase is not quite uniform, being greater at the 84 and 50 percentiles than at the 16 percentile level. Otherwise the figure shows no unusual or unexpected features.

THE SIX-DAY SAMPLE

As reported in Chapter IV, the children born on the first day of the even-numbered months of 1936, numbering 1,215, were each given an individual intelligence test, in addition to the group test. The group-test scores of 1,120 of these are known, the remainder being absent from school on the day of the group test. The question therefore is, how far are the 1,120 children in the six-day sample a good representation of the whole population of Scottish eleven-year-olds. The comparative scores for the six-day sample and for the whole survey group are given in Table XV.

TABLE XV

SIX-DAY SAMPLE AND ALL ELEVEN-YEAR-OLDS

| | All | | | Boys | | | Girls | | |
	N	Mean	S.D.	N	Mean	S.D.	N	Mean	S.D.
Six-Day Sample	1,120	37·27	15·96	545	36·83	16·88	575	37·70	15·02
Whole 1947 Survey	70,805	36·69	16·05	35,809	35·81	16·65	34,996	37·59	15·35

It will be noted that the values for the 1947 survey differ slightly from those appearing in Table X (p. 85). Since the 1932 test scores were presented in groups of ten, the 1947 scores, when being compared with the 1932 results, were also grouped in tens. The test scores of the six-day sample, however, have been arranged in groups of five, 0-4, 5-9, and so on; for the purpose of this comparison the scores of all the 1947 pupils have similarly been grouped in fives. The small discrepancies between the two sets of 1947 results are accordingly due to the different basis of computation.

At a first glance no great discrepancies between the means of the six-day sample and those for the whole survey are observable. The means of the two groups of boys differ by 1·02 points, this being the largest difference. To ascertain whether such differences indicate any real bias in the sample, various statistical tests of significance were applied to the data. None of the differences observed in Table XV was found to be significant. The difference between the boys' means is 1·40 times its standard error, and the difference between the means of the boys and girls combined, 0·58 points, is 1·20 times its standard error; all the other differences are less than their own standard error.[1] The distributions of the group-test scores of the sample were compared with those of the whole survey group by Dr D. N. Lawley, using the χ^2 (*chi* squared) technique; and again the differences were not significant.

Finally, the distribution of age by month of birth in the sample was compared with that for the whole group. The χ^2 test again showed no significant difference (P = ·25). As the median age of the sample is the same as that of the whole group, and the incidence of the dates of birth throughout the year for the sample is equivalent to that of the whole survey group, it follows that the comparisons between the test scores of the samples and all the survey can be made without any adjustments for age allowance. We have also seen that the test scores of the six-day sample do not significantly differ from those of the whole population tested. The six-day sample has, in fact,

[1] The ratio of the difference between two measures and the standard error of the difference indicates the probability of the difference being a chance one. The usual practice is to require such differences to be at least twice, and on stricter standards at least three times, their standard errors, before it can reasonably be assumed that chance factors are not operative.

been an adequately representative sample of the eleven-year-old population in respect of their verbal intelligence test scores. As the method of selecting the sample group for individual testing was the subject of considerable discussion when the 1947 survey was being planned, it is gratifying to find that the method of selection finally chosen has proved to be so satisfactory in practice.

THE ANSWER PATTERN

In *The Intelligence of Scottish Children* (pp. 87-8) appears a list of the number of times each item of the test was correctly answered by a group of 500 boys and 500 girls chosen at random. A similar table for 250 boys and 250 girls from the 1947 survey is presented below. Of each sex, 80 were taken from the cities and the remainder from the thirty-one counties, this being approximately the proportion of city and county pupils in the whole survey. Within these limits the scripts were chosen at random. The scripts so selected turn out to be those of a somewhat superior group, the mean score of 38·176 being higher than that of the whole survey group. This difference is, however, neither very large nor very significant, being, in fact, smaller than that for the 1932 group whose test scripts were analysed. In any case, this difference of mean has comparatively little bearing on the comparisons which can be based on the answer pattern. The only calculation which has been made so far on the data below is to estimate the reliability of the test. Using the Kuder-Richardson formula, the 1947 data give a reliability coefficient of $r = 0.94$, and the 1932 data give a corresponding value of $r = 0.95$. Though this value is exceeded by some of the more recently constructed group tests, it is by no means unsatisfactory for a test of this type.

No detailed comparison has been made of the answer patterns, but inspection of the 1947 and 1932 lists shows few divergences, and, indeed, a rather remarkable degree of correspondence.

ANSWER PATTERN (1947)

VERBAL TEST—NUMBER CORRECT

	Cities		Counties		
Question	Boys	Girls	Boys	Girls	All
1	75	73	147	151	446
2	69	72	141	165	447
3	31	37	69	89	226
4	73	76	142	153	444
5	58	56	128	146	388
6	62	66	124	152	404
7	57	66	128	159	410
8	50	45	128	135	358
9	33	37	75	112	257
10	45	59	87	110	301
11	57	62	139	155	413
12	59	60	141	158	418
13	60	62	133	147	402
14	50	52	112	126	340
15	39	48	107	120	314
16	60	68	128	137	393
17	26	24	37	55	142
18	22	10	23	23	78
19	39	47	85	117	288
20	31	23	74	88	216
21	62	70	130	145	407
22	30	37	68	93	228
23	50	49	100	120	319
24	57	58	116	152	383
25	53	57	109	147	366
26	22	27	58	87	194
27	14	18	55	47	134
28	20	14	43	42	119
29	41	50	95	113	299
30	26	23	59	67	175
31	60	61	134	147	402
32	58	52	122	147	379
33	56	58	122	145	381
34	38	30	66	60	194
35	17	24	44	58	143
36	58	62	122	147	389
37	32	44	70	113	259
38	26	30	66	90	212

Verbal Test—*continued*

Question	Cities		Counties		
	Boys	Girls	Boys	Girls	All
39	27	34	77	116	254
40	33	31	68	91	223
41	65	63	133	153	414
42	63	62	131	154	410
43	54	53	116	138	361
44a	39	31	64	95	229
44b	15	15	49	66	145
44c	17	10	40	38	105
45	39	38	89	85	251
46	26	28	77	70	201
47	20	26	50	51	147
48	27	22	58	62	169
49	60	61	128	151	400
50	38	43	86	111	278
51	12	12	35	35	94
52	40	45	85	110	280
53	19	19	52	64	154
54	50	57	114	142	363
55	33	50	73	113	269
56a	14	22	50	70	156
56b	48	39	104	99	290
56c	10	8	41	42	101
57	10	15	35	30	90
58	23	16	48	54	141
59	14	10	40	61	125
60	41	41	81	95	258
61	25	27	58	85	195
62	25	32	53	84	194
63	10	8	21	33	72
64	10	9	16	11	46
65	4	7	14	16	41
66a	6	8	14	32	60
66b	4	6	7	19	36
67	31	35	87	108	261
68	18	21	50	59	148
69	24	24	62	70	180
70	4	6	23	29	62
71	27	35	68	87	217
TOTAL	2,741	2,876	6,124	7,347	19,088
MEAN	34·26	35·95	36·02	43·22	38·176

PICTURE TEST—NUMBER CORRECT

Question	Cities		Counties		All
	Boys	Girls	Boys	Girls	
1	76	75	161	169	481
2	76	76	159	169	480
3	71	71	153	160	455
4	74	75	149	158	456
5	77	75	154	161	467
6	75	73	150	162	460
7	50	49	107	124	330
8	59	62	128	145	394
9	37	45	90	107	279
TOTAL	595	601	1,251	1,355	3,802
MEAN	7·44	7·51	7·36	7·97	7·60

Before concluding this chapter acknowledgment must be made of the assistance received from Miss C. Smith, M.A., and Messrs A. Nimmo and G. McKechnie in connection with operating the Hollerith counter-sorter at Moray House. Particular acknowledgment must also be made of the assistance given by Dr D. A. Walker, Deputy Director of Education for Fife. Most of the computations necessary in the preparation of this chapter were independently verified by Dr Walker.

VII

INTELLIGENCE AND FAMILY SIZE

THE object of this chapter is to present the data, as far as they are yet available, which have a bearing on the association of test score with size of family and with position in family. The conclusion seems unavoidable that family size and intelligence test score are negatively associated, but conclusions about the influence of position in family are tentative only and must be received with caution until more detailed analyses, especially of the thirty-six-day sample, are presented in a later volume.

Table XVI (pp. 102-6) gives, separately for boys and girls, the distribution of score in the group test for each position in each size of family. The scores are given in groups of five. The cases labelled YY are those children whose teachers certified that they could make no attempt at the test. These were classed, in calculations, together with the group of children scoring 0-4 marks. The cases labelled XX are absentees for whom, therefore, no group-test score is available. They were omitted in all calculations of mean score and the like.

From the details in Table XVI the mean group-test score can be calculated for each column, that is to say for each position in each size of family. This was done by centring each group of five points of score at its mid-point, the group 50-54, for example, at 52. The bottom group, 0-4, was thus centred at 2, so that the YY children, who were classed with this group, were thereby credited with a score of *two*. The top group is exceptional in that it contains seven points, 70-76. It was nevertheless centred at 72, partly to simplify the lengthy calculations, partly because in actual fact the top group contained few scores of 75 and 76. With these conventions the calculations give the results in Table XVII (p. 107).

TABLE XVI
GROUP-TEST SCORE BY SIZE OF FAMILY AND POSITION IN FAMILY

BOYS

Verbal Score	$\frac{1}{1}$	$\frac{1}{2}$	$\frac{2}{2}$	$\frac{1}{3}$	$\frac{2}{3}$	$\frac{3}{3}$	$\frac{1}{4}$	$\frac{2}{4}$	$\frac{3}{4}$	$\frac{4}{4}$	$\frac{1}{5}$	$\frac{2}{5}$	$\frac{3}{5}$	$\frac{4}{5}$	$\frac{5}{5}$
70-76	30	26	13	11	8	8	3	5		2					
65-69	144	153	100	46	43	35	17	20	14	17	7	4	4	7	6
60-64	253	333	205	132	93	89	48	36	50	44	4	9	9	17	14
55-59	402	441	364	232	188	166	76	65	77	72	20	24	28	35	47
50-54	537	644	437	325	236	230	131	113	102	120	35	45	66	60	56
45-49	525	650	460	374	309	279	144	180	133	146	57	56	77	86	81
40-44	478	604	422	376	315	247	176	183	177	164	59	97	89	102	102
35-39	385	485	379	311	296	219	164	159	197	136	69	116	99	114	103
30-34	310	379	245	253	273	187	124	167	156	147	65	101	114	106	76
25-29	259	272	205	183	197	148	107	111	131	108	60	72	83	79	90
20-24	185	211	169	137	142	113	91	113	134	86	43	74	71	75	61
15-19	132	162	130	138	138	100	79	92	106	69	34	64	64	63	48
10-14	124	123	90	90	92	93	63	86	69	54	20	48	66	48	35
5-9	98	120	71	74	104	72	64	58	65	39	28	46	47	40	49
0-4	83	94	72	86	90	76	39	61	58	58	25	52	40	41	44
YY	30	31	16	15	19	16	11	18	9	7	7	8	9	3	8
XX	183	259	155	179	133	118	83	83	73	90	30	54	61	49	54

Total 4,158 4,987 3,542 2,962 2,676 2,196 1,420 1,550 1,551 1,359 563 870 927 925 874

GIRLS

Verbal Score	$\frac{1}{1}$	$\frac{1}{2}$	$\frac{2}{2}$	$\frac{1}{3}$	$\frac{2}{3}$	$\frac{3}{3}$	$\frac{1}{4}$	$\frac{2}{4}$	$\frac{3}{4}$	$\frac{4}{4}$	$\frac{1}{5}$	$\frac{2}{5}$	$\frac{3}{5}$	$\frac{4}{5}$	$\frac{5}{5}$
70-76	16	31	17	6	7	4	1			2	1	1		1	
65-69	137	102	90	41	45	33	17	18	14	10	3	2	5	8	5
60-64	295	305	222	129	103	101	38	22	35	45	13	16	17	5	16
55-59	433	472	347	234	186	165	77	64	63	91	25	27	37	35	41
50-54	543	634	420	287	295	247	116	130	112	131	48	52	51	61	56
45-49	599	700	522	365	342	256	179	179	191	154	61	72	90	80	114
40-44	527	646	453	344	349	299	175	175	213	206	69	91	106	111	109
35-39	360	532	357	336	312	239	162	205	185	165	86	91	106	118	112
30-34	306	350	286	273	230	203	142	163	154	132	52	87	90	98	85
25-29	196	257	193	197	238	144	106	115	137	114	53	91	73	99	64
20-24	158	172	129	147	133	110	90	108	103	67	60	62	69	66	56
15-19	108	117	91	118	110	94	73	81	80	68	24	57	67	51	53
10-14	84	91	80	73	75	46	51	55	65	44	27	41	40	39	28
5-9	54	66	45	54	43	29	27	24	28	29	31	23	27	37	24
0-4	42	44	36	34	33	27	14	35	42	29	12	20	26	23	30
YY	18	13	17	20	15	13	7	14	8	11	2	10	5	11	6
XX	205	249	151	159	148	113	71	89	74	73	51	59	45	54	56

Total 4,081 4,781 3,456 2,817 2,664 2,123 1,346 1,477 1,504 1,371 618 802 854 897 855

TABLE XVI—*continued*

Boys

Verbal score	1/6	2/6	3/6	4/6	5/6	6/6	1/7	2/7	3/7	4/7	5/7	6/7	7/7	1/8	2/8	3/8	4/8	5/8	6/8	7/8	8/8
-76			1		1						1							1			
-69		1	3	1	3	5		1			1									1	
-64	2	3	9	10	4	8	1		3		4	5	5			1	3		4	2	2
-59	7	12	8	14	18	19	1	3	1	9	6	5	18	1	1	1	5	1	2	5	5
-54	9	28	26	27	24	34	9	12	12	18	9	10	27	2	1	2	9	5	11	15	9
-49	26	28	43	38	31	40	10	13	24	18	20	17	29	3	2	8	12	11	9	12	15
-44	25	37	53	58	62	57	7	15	25	30	16	28	44	2	5	10	15	23	19	15	22
-39	28	42	68	49	48	57	6	13	37	26	29	40	38		7	10	25	19	19	15	17
-34	27	38	55	55	61	66	4	12	32	48	37	32	23	2	5	12	17	20	27	23	18
-29	20	42	43	46	54	38	8	20	32	27	35	32	25		4	7	21	23	16	9	24
-24	16	31	28	45	38	51	12	17	39	32	21	29	28	1	1	12	15	17	10	7	11
-19	15	31	41	39	45	29	3	13	29	15	27	27	25	2	4	13	12	17	12	18	11
-14	17	33	41	28	28	30	9	5	18	20	17	24	24	3	2	5	15	11	12	10	9
-9	16	21	25	34	32	25	8	7	14	19	30	18	17	3	4	5	12	9	15	8	9
-4	11	22	32	36	30	26	2	7	19	19	30	19	19	6	9	8	12	16	25	17	13
Y	1	7	5	11	2	2	3	3	2	6	3	4			3	1	3	1	1	2	
XX	12	33	31	28	34	32	5	14	19	25	15	20	25		3	12	15	16	28	11	17
Total	232	409	512	519	515	519	88	155	306	312	301	310	347	27	48	109	189	191	211	169	184

Girls

Verbal score	1/6	2/6	3/6	4/6	5/6	6/6	1/7	2/7	3/7	4/7	5/7	6/7	7/7	1/8	2/8	3/8	4/8	5/8	6/8	7/8	8/8
-76	1		1																		
-69	1	3		2	3			2	1	2								1		1	1
-64	5	5	11	3	10	3	1		1	9	4		6		2	2	1	2		4	2
-59	3	13	16	17	14	17	2	7	5	10	2	7	7	1		2	1	2	2	5	5
-54	13	19	28	34	28	30	5	11	10	15	21	13	15	2	2	3	3	9	8	12	10
-49	25	32	45	35	40	58	9	10	13	19	25	31	33	1	4	5	13	16	17	16	16
-44	26	46	63	61	68	68	14	11	19	31	37	30	37	2	6	10	14	16	26	24	26
-39	24	39	64	72	61	69	7	18	28	44	43	39	39	1	3	10	25	23	29	26	31
-34	23	29	63	59	70	62	8	25	31	32	40	44	37	6	9	12	21	37	23	22	23
-29	27	35	57	53	36	57	7	17	25	28	36	35	29	1	3	10	19	16	14	21	16
-24	15	42	33	38	54	38	8	12	25	22	34	22	22	1	4	10	14	27	26	18	13
-19	16	23	34	32	32	36	5	17	26	17	18	24	19	4	6	8	7	15	12	14	15
-14	6	23	26	39	27	23	1	8	13	23	30	15	17		4	8	17	13	15	7	10
-9	14	14	22	22	22	23	2	7	20	14	20	17	14	2	2	4	8	11	9	12	6
-4	8	16	17	19	18	16	2	5	12	12	18	13	8	2	4	7	7	8	12	6	8
Y		5	2	7	4	6		2	1	5	3	4	2	1		2	1	2	2	2	2
XX	15	29	29	36	26	43	4	9	20	29	11	32	28	2	5	5	14	19	14	8	9
Total	222	373	510	530	513	549	75	161	250	312	342	326	313	26	54	95	167	216	212	193	193

TABLE XVI—*continued*

Boys

Verbal Score	1/9	2/9	3/9	4/9	5/9	6/9	7/9	8/9	9/9	1/10	2/10	3/10	4/10	5/10	6/10	7/10	8/10	9/10	10/10	3/11	4/11
70-76													1								
65-69								1	1												
60-64	1	1		1	1	1			2				1							1	
55-59				2	5	1	1		2				1		1	2	1	3			
50-54		1	1	2	6	5			2						1	3	3	3			1
45-49			1	7	5	10	5	5					4	5	1	1	3	6			1
40-44	1	3	4	11	11	9	4	8			1		2	4	4	4	3	5	4		
35-39		1	1	8	15	17	9	7	15		1	1	7	7	1	5	6	1	5	1	1
30-34	1	2	2	3	14	8	10	8	5			3	4	8	8	5	8	2	4		
25-29	1	1	4	8	12	6	10	16	13			3	1	4	5	7	8	7	5		
20-24	1	1	5	6	12	10	6	6	6				1	5	4	4	7	6	3		2
15-19	1	2	5	8	4	12	12	11	7	1	1	1	7	4	3	6	3	4			1
10-14			4	5	10	12	6	3	8			1	5	2	5	5	1	1			1
5-9			2	5	5	12	8	8	11	1	1	2	6	3	5	4	3	2			
0-4		1	6	7	11	6	17	8	3				2	4	6	4	9	2	5	2	2
YY			1		2	2	1	2						1	1	3		1			1
XX	1		2	4	11	7	10	2	9		1	1	4	3	9	3	2	5	1		
Total	7	13	33	60	119	120	115	82	97	1	3	11	21	62	46	57	65	40	51	4	10

Girls

Verbal Score	1/9	2/9	3/9	4/9	5/9	6/9	7/9	8/9	9/9	1/10	2/10	3/10	4/10	5/10	6/10	7/10	8/10	9/10	10/10	1/11	2/11	3/11	4/11
70-76				1																			
65-69																							
60-64			1				1	1	5								1		3				
55-59	1		1	1		6	2	1	7								1	2	2				
50-54	2			1	5	6	2	4	12			2		2	1	3	4	4	1				1
45-49	1	3	4	6	11	3	11	6	14			1		5	5	3	5	3				1	
40-44		3	3	6	11	10	11	20	8		2		4	5	3	6	9	1	6				2
35-39	1	1	4	11	14	10	15	22	17	1		3	3	8	5	9	7	4				1	
30-34			3	1	14	13	9	13	19			3	4	6	5	5	9	8	11				
25-29		3	2	10	13	15	14	9	9			1	4	9	8	12	8	5					2
20-24		3	5	4	9	15	8	6	15		2	2	5	7	4	5	7	4				1	3
15-19		3	4	4	11	8	10	17	5	1	3	4	4	5	3	3	3	6					1
10-14	3	2	3	7	7	7	3	11	5	1				7	10	5	4	5	3		1		2
5-9	1	3	5	4	7	7	3	4	4		1	2	4	3	2	5	4	1					1
0-4			1	1	8	7	7	2	5		1	4	1	1	10	2	2	5		1			
YY				1			1	1															
XX	1	2	3	5	10	6	10	9	3		2	2	3	10	6	6	1	3	1				1
Total	10	23	39	61	122	114	106	126	129	3	2	14	27	44	67	62	73	57	57	1	3	3	12

TABLE XVI—*continued*

Boys

Verbal Score	5/11	6/11	7/11	8/11	9/11	10/11	11/11	4/12	5/12	6/12	7/12	8/12	9/12	10/12	11/12	12/12	4/13	5/13	6/13	7/13	8/13	9/13	10/13	11/13	12/13	13/13
70-76																										
65-69				I																						
60-64													I													
55-59				I	I	I						I														
50-54	I		I	I	3					I	I		I	2						I						
45-49		2		4	2	4				I		I	I	I	4						I					
40-44	2	I	2	2	5	2	I			I	I	I	2		I	I										
35-39	2	3	2	4	I	I	I					I	3	3	2	I						2		I		
30-34	I	2	2	6	I	5	4	I		I	3	2	I	I	I							I	I	I		
25-29	4	I	4	2	2	4				I	2	2	3	2		I				2		I	I			
20-24	2	2	5	2	I						I	2	I	I	I	I			I	I		I	I	I		
15-19	2		I	I		I			2	5	4	I	3	I				I	I		2	I		I	3	
10-14	I	2	4	3	I	4				I	3	I		I	I	2										
5-9	I	3	3	I	I		2			2	I		2	2	I		I	2			I	2	I			I
0-4	2	6	2	5	4	4				3	2	2		3	I						I		I	I		
YY					I																					
XX	2		3	I	3	I				I	I		4	I				I		I	I		I		I	
Total	9	20	26	30	29	23	29	1	1	14	19	16	18	15	14	13	1	4	4	2	6	7	6	5	5	1

Girls

Verbal Score	5/11	6/11	7/11	8/11	9/11	10/11	11/11	4/12	5/12	6/12	7/12	8/12	9/12	10/12	11/12	12/12	4/13	5/13	6/13	7/13	8/13	9/13	10/13	11/13	12/13	13/13
70-76																										
65-69		I																								
60-64		I											I									I				I
55-59			I		2								I													
50-54	I	I	2	3	2								I	I		I						2		I		
45-49	I	3	4	2	I	2									2	2					I				I	I
40-44	2	4	2	2	3	4	2						2	I	I	I				I	I					3
35-39	I	5	5	2	4	3		I	2	I		I		2	I	I				2		I	I		I	I
30-34	2	3	4	6	4	3	I	I		I		2	4	I	I	2		I		3	2	2		3		I
25-29	I	3	5	5		2	3		I	2		I	2	3		2			I		2			I		4
20-24	4	2	2	2	I	I	2	I		I	2	I	2	I	I	I	3					2	I		I	
15-19	I	2		3	I	2	3			I	I	2	I	3	I	I									I	
10-14	3	I	2	3	3	I					2	I		2	I	3					I					
5-9	2	I		2	3	I	I				2		I	2		I		I			2	I	I	I	I	
0-4		I	2	I	3	I	I				2		I		2	I		I			2					
YY					I								I			I										
XX		2	I	2		2	2			I	I		2	2							I				I	I
Total	18	25	31	35	24	21	22	1	3	10	12	9	18	13	14	11	13	1	2	8	12	6	6	4	6	12

TABLE XVI—*continued*

BOYS

*Family size 14   (6) 27, (7) 12, 12, 2, 2, (8) 37, 22, 2,
                   (10) 37, 17, 12, 2, (11) 2, (12) 42, 32, 2, 2,
                   (13) 42, 27, 27, 7, 2, (14) 22, 22;
Family size 15   (8) 27, 17, 7, (10) 27, (11) 22, 7, (12) 2;
Family size 16   (6) 17, (9) 17, (10) 32, (12) 32;
Family size 17   (13) 2, (17) 17;
Family size 18   (17) 7;
Family size 19   (19) YY.

GIRLS

*Family size 14   (5) 27, (6) 22, (7) YY, (8) 22, (9) 22,
                   (10) 37, 37, (11) 32, 7, (12) 42, 2, (13) 37;
Family size 15   (7) 17, (8) 57, 22, (9) 12, (10) xx, (11) xx,
                   (12) 2, (14) 17;
Family size 16   (5) 42, (6) 2, (9) 12, (10) 17, (11) 47,
                   (14) 27, (15) 52;
Family size 17   (11) 17, (12) 37.

* The figure in the bracket denotes the position in the family. Thus in families of fifteen (boys) the three eighth children score 27, 17, 7, the tenth child scores 27, the two eleventh children 22, 7, and the twelfth child 2.

SUMMARY OF TABLE XVI

Verbal Score	BOYS Size and Position Known	Unknown	GIRLS Size and Position Known	Unknown
70-76	111		90	
65-69	636	2	548	2
60-64	1,412	7	1,449	6
55-59	2,402	14	2,463	7
50-54	3,477	26	3,540	21
45-49	4,041	24	4,471	39
40-44	4,261	24	4,649	27
35-39	3,963	32	4,236	37
30-34	3,458	40	3,499	32
25-29	2,781	26	2,783	19
20-24	2,278	21	2,148	23
15-19	1,975	27	1,694	22
10-14	1,558	22	1,275	14
5-9	1,415	18	891	15
0-4	1,439	25	744	19
YY	284	10	229	9
XX	2,096	93	2,090	122
	37,587	411	36,799	414

TABLE XVII

Mean Group-Test Score for each Position in each Size of Family

Position Size	Boys No.	Omit xx cases	Nett No.	Total Score	Girls No.	Omit xx cases	Nett No.	Total Score	Boys and Girls Nett No.	Total Score	Mean Score	All Positions in Family
1/1	4,158	183	3,975	162,955	4,081	205	3,876	167,047	7,851	330,002	42·03	
												42·03
1/2	4,987	259	4,728	194,691	4,781	249	4,532	193,144	9,260	387,835	41·88	
2/2	3,542	155	3,387	138,529	3,456	151	3,305	139,535	6,692	278,064	41·55	
												41·74
1/3	2,962	179	2,783	107,256	2,817	159	2,658	104,131	5,441	211,387	38·85	
2/3	2,676	133	2,543	92,491	2,664	148	2,516	98,002	5,059	190,493	37·65	
3/3	2,196	118	2,078	77,421	2,123	113	2,010	79,680	4,088	157,101	38·43	
												38·32
1/4	1,420	83	1,337	47,209	1,346	71	1,275	47,215	2,612	94,424	36·15	
2/4	1,550	83	1,467	49,529	1,477	89	1,388	49,326	2,855	98,855	34·63	
3/4	1,551	73	1,478	49,491	1,504	74	1,430	50,620	2,908	100,021	34·40	
4/4	1,359	90	1,269	44,873	1,371	73	1,298	48,341	2,567	93,214	36·31	
												35·32
1/5	563	30	533	17,111	618	51	567	19,339	1,100	36,450	33·14	
2/5	870	54	816	24,442	802	59	743	24,301	1,559	48,743	31·27	
3/5	927	61	866	26,632	854	45	809	26,993	1,675	53,625	32·01	
4/5	925	49	876	28,372	897	54	843	27,796	1,719	56,168	32·67	
5/5	874	54	820	26,650	855	56	799	27,813	1,619	54,463	33·64	
												32·51
1/6	232	12	220	6,650	222	15	207	6,704	427	13,354	31·27	
2/6	409	33	376	10,977	373	29	344	10,723	720	21,700	30·14	
3/6	512	31	481	14,377	510	29	481	15,542	962	29,919	31·10	
4/6	519	28	491	14,247	530	36	494	15,373	985	29,620	30·07	
5/6	515	34	481	14,267	513	26	487	15,534	968	29,801	30·79	
6/6	519	32	487	15,409	549	43	506	16,302	993	31,711	31·93	
												30·88
1/7	88	5	83	2,406	75	4	71	2,442	154	4,848	31·48	
2/7	155	14	141	4,232	161	9	152	4,674	293	8,906	30·40	
3/7	306	19	287	8,009	250	20	230	6,360	517	14,369	27·79	
4/7	312	25	287	8,164	312	29	283	8,826	570	16,990	29·81	
5/7	301	15	286	7,412	342	11	331	9,622	617	17,034	27·61	
6/7	310	20	290	8,015	326	32	294	8,813	584	16,828	28·81	
7/7	347	25	322	10,254	313	28	285	9,195	607	19,449	32·04	
												29·45
1/8	27	0	27	629	26	2	24	658	51	1,287	25·24	
2/8	48	3	45	1,100	54	5	49	1,408	94	2,508	26·68	
3/8	109	12	97	2,564	95	5	90	2,510	187	5,074	27·13	
4/8	189	15	174	4,993	167	14	153	4,346	327	9,339	28·56	
5/8	191	16	175	4,660	216	19	197	5,764	372	10,424	28·02	
6/8	211	28	183	4,951	212	14	198	5,826	381	10,777	28·29	
7/8	169	11	158	4,656	193	8	185	5,750	343	10,406	30·34	
8/8	184	17	167	4,989	193	9	184	5,878	351	10,867	30·96	
												28·81
1/9	7	1	6	202	10	1	9	288	15	490	32·67	
2/9	13	0	13	426	23	2	21	547	34	973	28·62	
3/9	33	2	31	532	39	3	36	982	67	1,514	22·60	
4/9	60	4	56	1,252	61	5	56	1,622	112	2,874	25·66	
5/9	119	11	108	2,911	122	10	112	3,219	220	6,130	27·86	
6/9	120	7	113	3,071	114	6	108	3,021	221	6,092	27·57	
7/9	115	10	105	2,650	106	10	96	2,897	201	5,547	27·60	
8/9	82	2	80	1,905	126	9	117	3,509	197	5,414	27·48	
9/9	97	9	88	2,476	129	3	126	4,322	214	6,798	31·77	
												27·97
10	357	28	329	8,603	406	33	373	10,306	702	18,909	26·94	
11	180	11	169	4,303	195	11	184	5,348	353	9,651	27·34	
12	111	8	103	2,626	104	8	96	2,427	199	5,053	25·39	
over 12	80	4	76	1,387	86	5	81	2,257	157	3,644	23·21	

The fall in mean test score with increasing size of family is very evident from the foregoing tables: it is even more clearly seen when shown as a descending graph.

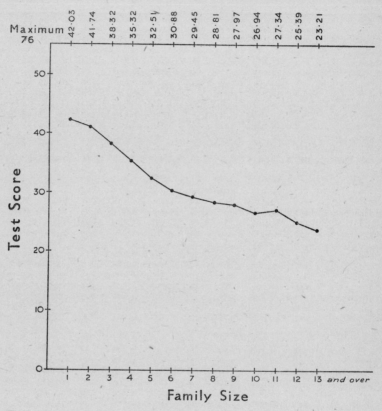

Fig. 5.   Mean Score in Group Test of Families of Different Sizes

The establishment of this association does not, of course, decide what its cause is, whether, for example, the larger families tend to be unintelligent because they are large, or to be large because their parents are not intelligent. The richer data of the thirty-six-day sample may throw some light on this when they are analysed. Some day a sufficiently wide survey may be undertaken, in which the intelligence of parents is also estimated, but we did not venture to attempt this. One hypothesis which has been advanced to explain the fall of score with increasing size of family we can, however, begin to investigate from our tables, namely, the hypothesis that later-born children in families tend to be less intelligent. This would not only explain the lower scores of large families, but, if families are now smaller, might also explain a rise in the average score of the whole population, such as we have found.

Past evidence about intelligence and position in family is scanty and conflicting, chiefly because the influence of position is so difficult to disentangle from the influence of size of family. First-born children exist in all families, fifth-born children only in large families.

Our data, however, permit us to examine the influence of position separately for each size of family. The mean scores for each position are shown in Table XVII. A first inspection of that table does not suggest that position in the family has much to do with intelligence. At least there is no immediate evidence of a fall in intelligence in late-born children such as would explain the striking and steady fall with increasing size of family. There is certainly a strong suggestion that the first-born is a little more intelligent than those in the middle of the family, but there is equally a suggestion in the figures that the last-born also is more intelligent. The first-born and the last-born have higher mean scores than the others in all the family sizes except size eight. When curves are drawn separately for each family, they are for the most part slightly concave upwards. Whether this is statistically significant or not has been investigated by Dr. Lawley, separately for boys and girls. The variances and standard errors are shown in Table XVIII up to families of size four, beyond which the numbers become small, and the difficulty about unfinished families becomes acute.

TABLE XVIII

Boys

Position in Family	Number of Cases	Mean	Standard Error	Variance
1/1	3,975	40·99	0·26	261·52
1/2	4,728	41·18	0·23	250·36
2/2	3,387	40·90	0·27	244·48
1/3	2,783	38·54	0·31	251·48
2/3	2,543	36·37	0·32	263·97
3/3	2,078	37·26	0·36	274·21
1/4	1,337	35·31	0·44	260·42
2/4	1,467	33·76	0·42	262·94
3/4	1,478	33·42	0·41	250·29
4/4	1,269	35·36	0·45	257·29

Girls

Position in Family	Number of Cases	Mean	Standard Error	Variance
1/1	3,876	43·10	0·24	214·76
1/2	4,532	42·62	0·21	198·86
2/2	3,305	42·22	0·25	210·25
1/3	2,658	39·18	0·29	219·32
2/3	2,516	38·95	0·30	212·89
3/3	2,010	39·64	0·32	211·06
1/4	1,275	37·03	0·40	207·97
2/4	1,388	35·54	0·39	210·80
3/4	1,430	35·40	0·39	213·73
4/4	1,298	37·24	0·41	220·12

Dr. Lawley calls attention to the fact that the variances for boys are very strikingly larger than those for girls. He continues: "In the case of families of size three there are for the girls no significant differences between the means for different positions. For the boys, however, the mean of 38·54 for 1/3 is significantly (at 1% level) greater than the other two; the difference between the means for 2/3 and 3/3 is nearly, but not quite, significant at the 5% level.

As regards families of size four, both for boys and

for girls the means for 1/4 and 4/4 are each significantly greater at the 1% level than the means for either 2/4 or 3/4."

The data just as they stand, however, are open to the objection that the different positions in a family are not equally fairly sampled. All our children were eleven years of age. Therefore first-born, and early-born, children are necessarily under-represented in the larger families. In families of seven, for example, we have only 154 first-borns, but 607 seventh children. Furthermore, there seems reason to suspect that parents of eleven-year-old children in different positions in the family may not be equally intelligent samples of all parents. Consider families of size five. The *last*-born of a family of five, now aged eleven, is a member of what is very probably a completed family, which may also, for all we know, be well-spaced. His parents, therefore, may very well be intelligent parents who have planned their family, and his own intelligence may be inherited from them. The third-born of such a family, if he is one of our age group, has two older and two younger sibs. The family may still, for all we know, be a well-spaced and completed family, born to thoughtful parents. But consider next the *first*-born of five, in our group. Here we have a child aged eleven with four younger sibs. The family may very well not be finished, may be going to be far larger in due time. And the children can be only about two years apart. In short, it may well be that the " first-borns " of any of our larger families are representative, on the whole, of less intelligent parents, and this would upset our first conclusion that intelligence and position are not associated, or only very slightly associated. The slight concavity of our curves, in fact, could be explained by the two assumptions, (*a*) that early-born children do tend to be more intelligent, and (*b*) that intelligent parents of well-spaced and definitely completed families are most adequately represented, *in our data,* among the later-born children of any given size of family.

Other hypotheses will occur to the reader. For example, youngest-born in our data, being eleven years of age, possibly have older brethren at work and bringing in a wage which increases the possibility of the home being a favourable educational background: or they may have left the home and reduced the family, in effect, to a smaller size. Indeed, one can imagine that the *first*-born are more favoured because the home is not yet crowded, the *last*-born because it has ceased to be crowded.

Again, the last-born of our families are on the whole the children of older mothers, that is, the children of a slightly earlier generation, and their superiority may indeed be evidence of a fall in general intelligence as the generations succeed one another.

But all these hypotheses are highly speculative, and are only possibilities to be kept in mind as we proceed with the further analysis of our data, most of the information in which has not yet been correlated with the test scores.

The average size of family of all the above 70,200 children for whom we have a group-test score can be readily calculated from the tables, and is 3·735. The average family for the 4,186 children who were absent (the XX cases) is 4·061. It is probable, therefore, that they would have slightly reduced the general average score had they worked the test, but we have no reason to think that these absentees differed, either in quantity or quality, from the absentees of 1932. Taking the 70,200 and the 4,186 children all together, the average family size is 3·753.

To prevent any misunderstanding, however, it must be at once emphasized that 3·753 is not in any sense an estimate of the size of Scottish families, for several reasons, all arising from the fact that it is derived from a year group of children. In the first place, childless families are totally unrepresented, and were they included the average size would fall considerably. On the other hand, a number of our families are certain to be unfinished. Thirdly, the parents of these children are not of one definite generation but are of all sorts of ages. Most important perhaps of all is the fact that in a complete year group large families are over-represented in exact proportion to their size. An only child can occur in only one year group, a large family is represented in many year groups. This over-representation of the large families means that our actual average size, 3·753, is far larger than the average size of all Scottish families, which is probably well below three. We hesitate to deduce any estimate from our data; it is indeed impossible to do so, and this paragraph is only inserted here lest some reader should hastily draw erroneous conclusions. A year group is an excellent sample for estimating the intelligence of a generation of children. It is a bad sample from which to deduce average family size, and we have not attempted this.

THE SIX-DAY SAMPLE

The individual testing of the six-day sample supports the group-test observation that mean score falls with increasing size of family. For the 1,110 children for whom we have both a group-test score and a Terman-Merrill IQ and also family size and position in family, the following are the mean figures:

Family Size	Number	Group-Test Score	Terman-Merrill IQ
1	115	43·4	113
2	267	41·4	109
3	235	39·7	105
4	178	36·7	101
5	109	31·4	96
6	77	29·2	91
7	63	30·0	93
8	28	28·2	91
9	18	26·8	91
10 and over	20	32·0	95

In this six-day sample the numbers are hardly sufficient to justify comparing the different positions. However, for what they are worth, the following are the facts:

	MEAN TERMAN-MERRILL IQs					
Family Size			Position in Family			
	1	2	3	4	5	6
2	108(156)	110(111)				
3	108(90)	103(88)	104(57)			
4	99(41)	102(50)	98(49)	106(38)		
5	92(24)	96(17)	92(29)	99(20)	102(19)	
6	85(9)	96(12)	94(19)	85(9)	97(15)	84(13)

The figures in brackets give the number of cases. There is here no evidence that the first-born are superior, but some that the last-born are.

CORRELATION COEFFICIENTS

Since in many previous articles the negative association between test score and size of family has been expressed by a correlation coefficient, the necessary grids are given here to enable such to be calculated for our data. But it should be remarked that, in view of the skewness of the grids, the correlation coefficient is not a very appropriate statistic to use. The coefficients are somewhat higher than usual, and that for the Terman-Merrill individual test (which is probably more free from schooling) is higher than that for the group test.

Also tables are given on pp. 116-7 showing the distributions over the months of the year of (a) size of family and (b) position in family.

TABLE XIX

CORRELATION BETWEEN GROUP-TEST SCORE AND SIZE OF FAMILY
BOYS AND GIRLS

Verbal Score	1	2	3	4	5	6	7	8	9	10	11	12	13+	
70-76	46	87	44	13	3	4	1	1	1	1				201
65-69	281	445	243	127	51	22	7	4	2	2				1,184
60-64	548	1,065	647	318	120	73	39	25	15	6	1	3	1	2,861
55-59	835	1,624	1,171	585	319	158	83	37	31	13	6	2	1	4,865
50-54	1,080	2,135	1,620	955	530	300	187	103	50	27	17	8	5	7,017
45-49	1,124	2,332	1,925	1,306	774	441	271	160	92	42	27	13	5	8,512
40-44	1,005	2,125	1,930	1,469	935	624	344	235	123	63	36	12	9	8,910
35-39	745	1,753	1,713	1,373	1,014	621	407	260	168	74	37	19	15	8,199
30-34	616	1,269	1,419	1,185	874	608	405	277	125	93	44	22	20	6,957
25-29	455	927	1,107	929	764	508	356	206	146	87	38	22	19	5,564
20-24	343	681	782	792	637	429	323	187	118	66	32	19	17	4,426
15-19	240	500	698	648	525	373	265	170	124	62	19	26	19	3,669
10-14	208	384	469	487	392	321	224	141	96	55	32	18	6	2,833
5-9	152	302	376	334	352	270	207	119	89	49	22	15	19	2,306
and YY	173	323	444	421	382	303	223	181	101	64	40	20	21	2,696
Total existing xx	7,851	15,952	14,588	10,942	7,672	5,055	3,342	2,106	1,281	702	353	199	157	70,200

$$r = -0.28$$

TABLE XX

CORRELATION BETWEEN TERMAN-MERILL IQ AND SIZE OF FAMILY
SIX-DAY SAMPLE

BOYS AND GIRLS

IQ	1	2	3	4	5	6	7	8	9	10	11+	
170+	1	1	1									3
160-9	2	3		1								6
150-9	3	6	3	1								13
140-9	9	8	9	3	1		1					31
130-9	15	20	11	5	3	1	1	1	1			58
120-9	15	35	27	12	6	2	3	2	1		2	105
110-9	16	47	38	24	8	4	4	1	1	2	1	146
100-9	24	57	49	47	21	8	9	2	1	1	2	221
90-9	10	49	44	46	27	24	17	7	3	2	3	232
80-9	10	21	35	22	24	22	14	8	8	1	1	166
70-9	7	15	15	12	14	14	11	6	1	1	3	99
60-9	3	5	2	5	3	1	3	1	2	1		26
50-9			1		2	1						4
	115	267	235	178	109	77	63	28	18	8	12	1,110

$$r = -0.32$$

TABLE XXI

DISTRIBUTION OF SIZE OF FAMILY BY MONTH OF BIRTH

BOYS

Size of Family	Jan.	Feb.	Mar.	Apr.	May	June	July	Aug.	Sept.	Oct.	Nov.	Dec.	Total
1	343	313	379	364	382	351	369	326	351	328	346	306	4,158
2	715	656	788	738	754	767	680	723	674	698	633	658	8,52(
3	626	651	731	731	664	661	648	595	636	634	626	631	7,834
4	509	457	525	534	556	513	470	474	468	435	453	486	5,88(
5	361	340	396	357	355	361	325	365	320	339	312	328	4,159
6	231	220	245	240	274	202	214	200	228	225	213	214	2,70(
7	165	137	176	161	183	180	147	146	115	133	127	149	1,81(
8	101	107	110	103	99	90	77	110	81	82	76	92	1,128
9	47	65	58	73	56	54	55	49	43	53	45	48	64(
10	31	29	39	25	31	32	28	24	27	34	34	23	357
11	7	15	13	21	17	15	11	16	15	14	15	21	18(
12	5	13	10	9	10	12	11	9	6	13	17	6	11(
13	5	2	4	1	9	2	4	2	3	5	3	1	4(
14	1	4	2	2	2	4	1	3	2	1	2		2(
15		1	1							1	2	2	7
16				1			1	1				1	4
17				1			1						2
18	1												1
19					1								1
Unknown	38	32	37	48	30	36	29	28	31	41	31	30	411
	3,186	3,042	3,514	3,455	3,422	3,280	3,071	3,071	3,000	3,036	2,923	2,998	37,998

GIRLS

Size of Family	Jan.	Feb.	Mar.	Apr.	May	June	July	Aug.	Sept.	Oct.	Nov.	Dec.	Total
1	324	299	344	365	387	373	343	346	313	322	348	317	4,081
2	683	634	761	762	726	742	655	662	624	663	631	694	8,237
3	618	608	703	676	695	645	623	624	574	630	602	606	7,604
4	449	454	531	508	534	505	495	480	434	450	436	422	5,698
5	362	337	345	349	356	347	350	304	306	345	300	325	4,026
6	255	243	260	218	221	217	229	220	219	173	215	227	2,697
7	158	155	152	164	165	166	139	139	148	135	103	155	1,779
8	92	84	117	108	100	113	109	90	83	85	87	88	1,156
9	86	60	73	57	68	50	73	47	37	57	69	53	730
10	30	28	29	33	45	41	30	34	39	30	27	40	406
11	12	10	26	24	14	20	15	13	16	16	18	11	195
12	7	10	6	11	7	10	5	7	12	12	11	6	104
13	8	5	3	7	7	2	4	2	5	4	4	6	57
14	3	1		1	1	1	2	1		2			12
15	1		1		1	1		2					8
16		1						1			3	2	7
17										1		1	2
Unknown	26	53	38	34	39	31	22	39	30	28	39	35	414
	3,114	2,981	3,390	3,317	3,366	3,264	3,094	3,011	2,841	2,957	2,893	2,985	37,213

TABLE XXII

Distribution of Position in Family by Month of Birth

Boys

Position in Family	Jan.	Feb.	Mar.	Apr.	May	June	July	Aug.	Sept.	Oct.	Nov.	Dec.	Total
1	1,236	1,121	1,323	1,336	1,310	1,235	1,162	1,152	1,175	1,152	1,132	1,111	14,445
2	757	716	879	801	845	827	749	760	729	746	738	719	9,266
3	461	509	533	548	462	465	470	446	438	447	398	472	5,649
4	296	269	285	291	311	297	292	298	259	261	245	293	3,397
5	158	175	191	188	202	163	157	175	179	176	168	144	2,076
6	119	94	123	106	111	116	89	103	84	104	103	94	1,246
7	63	64	72	68	72	70	71	53	44	51	46	65	739
8	29	30	33	31	39	36	24	29	32	32	34	40	389
9	13	18	22	22	23	16	15	11	16	6	10	20	192
10	9	9	9	7	10	10	7	7	10	10	7	6	101
11	3	5	6	4	4	3	1	5	1	6	9	3	51
12	2	2	2	2	2	4	2	2	2	4	1		24
13				1			1	2		1		1	7
14					1	1							2
17	1			1									2
19				1									1
Unknown	38	32	37	48	30	36	29	28	31	41	31	30	411
	3,186	3,042	3,514	3,455	3,422	3,280	3,071	3,071	3,000	3,036	2,923	2,998	37,998

Girls

Position in Family	Jan.	Feb.	Mar.	Apr.	May	June	July	Aug.	Sept.	Oct.	Nov.	Dec.	Total
1	1,156	1,074	1,265	1,261	1,299	1,244	1,114	1,106	1,064	1,131	1,143	1,124	13,981
2	762	746	834	784	808	789	748	760	680	707	674	723	9,015
3	424	442	495	499	471	470	469	456	414	437	382	433	5,392
4	279	272	314	291	302	271	314	264	283	269	255	266	3,380
5	199	167	205	183	186	193	167	165	140	162	174	181	2,212
6	115	113	97	120	127	115	114	100	103	107	104	94	1,309
7	77	58	69	71	50	60	59	56	63	50	51	60	724
8	36	23	35	34	55	58	53	34	32	34	32	33	459
9	25	17	23	22	15	17	18	13	17	15	25	25	232
10	7	9	12	11	11	12	2	10	10	4	8	6	102
11	3	2	4	3		2	6	6	2	6	4	4	42
12	3	3		2	1	2	3	1	3	3		2	23
13	2	1		2	2		3	1		1		2	15
14											2		2
15		1											1
Unknown	26	54	36	34	39	31	24	39	30	29	39	33	414
	3,114	2,981	3,390	3,317	3,366	3,264	3,094	3,011	2,841	2,957	2,893	2,985	37,213

K

VIII

COMPARISON OF THE 1947 AND 1932
INDIVIDUAL TEST RESULTS

IN her introduction to *The Intelligence of a Representative Group of Scottish Children,* Dr A. M. Macmeeken writes: " During the planning of the Mental Survey by the Scottish Council for Research in Education . . . the late Dr Shepherd Dawson insisted on the importance of testing individually a representative sample of pupils so that the results of the group test used in the survey might be satisfactorily calibrated and converted into intelligence quotients." Thus to one of the most able and clear-sighted educational psychologists of our generation is due much of the credit for devising what up to the present appears to be the ideal form for a survey of this kind: namely, the group testing of a very large sample combined with the individual testing of a random sub-sample drawn from it. In accordance with this plan 500 boys and 500 girls, the Binet Thousand, selected from the pupils group-tested in 1932, were also tested on the Stanford Revision. Owing to the fact that the verbal scores were known for these 1000 children and for the whole age group, and thanks to the high correlation between the two tests, it was possible to calculate relatively reliable mean Stanford IQs for the eleven-year-old Scottish children of 1932, as is fully described in *The Intelligence of Scottish Children.*

The six-day sample of 1947 was composed of pupils tested on the verbal group test and on the Terman-Merrill Revision of the Binet scale, as is described in Chapter IV of the present volume. This permits the calculation of estimates of the mean Terman-Merrill IQ for eleven-year-old Scottish pupils of 1947. It is unfortunate that a different revision had to be used in the second survey; this was unavoidable, however, owing to shortage of test material and of testers experienced in the administration of the earlier revision. In order to compare the Binet IQ level of 1947 with that of 1932 it is necessary, therefore, to convert Terman-Merrill IQs into Stanford IQs (or vice versa). For this purpose results are available for the eighty-nine children tested on both revisions, as given in Appendix I, p. 59. It is hoped to increase this number considerably, but it seemed essential that in the meantime the present volume should include at least some attempt to determine whether there has been any change in Binet IQ level during the fifteen years that have elapsed between the two surveys. As shown below, it does seem possible, owing to the very high correlation between the IQs on the two revisions, to make useful estimates, and it is encouraging to find that the consequences of using different revisions are not as serious as might perhaps have been anticipated.

THE RELATION OF VERBAL SCORE AND TERMAN-MERRILL IQ: 1947 SURVEY

Tables XXIII and XXIV show the verbal group-test scores and the Terman-Merrill IQs of the 545 boys and 575 girls comprising the six-day sample. The omission of those pupils who were absent from the group test accounts for certain slight discrepancies between the figures of Chapter IV and those of the present chapter. The IQs are age-corrected, the verbal scores are not; time has not permitted this. No doubt the association with age-corrected verbal scores would be somewhat closer, but as the spread in chronological age is only one year, any improvement would be slight. The procedure of this chapter is, of course, uniform; raw verbal scores are used throughout.

TABLE XXIII

VERBAL SCORE AND TERMAN-MERRILL IQ
SIX-DAY SAMPLE, 1947 SURVEY

BOYS

Terman-Merrill IQ (group centres)

	52	57	62	67	72	77	82	87	92	97	102	107	112	117	122	127	132	137	142	147	152	157	162	167	172	
72																							I	2		3
67																I	I	I	2	I	I	I	I			9
62								*		2	I	2	3	2	6	I	5	2	I	2	I	I				29
57									2	3	2	3	8	11	7	4	2	4	I							47
52								I	2	2	6	9	11	5	7	5	4	I								53
47								3	I	14	11	13	7	9	6	2	I	I								68
42							I	3	6	10	14	7	6	I	I											49
37							2	8	13	11	7	7	2	I												51
32					2	I	4	6	9	16	13	3				I										55
27				I	7	7	8	7	9	8	5	2	I	I												56
22					I	2	6	10	I	5	3	3	I													32
17					2	5	3	4	7	2	I		I													25
12				I	3	4	2	9	2	I		2														24
7				2	3	4		3	I	6	I															20
2	2	2	4	3	5	3	I	2	I					I												24
	0	2	2	8	14	28	27	41	43	63	66	53	47	32	28	29	21	11	9	8	3	3	2	3	2	545

TABLE XXIV

VERBAL SCORE AND TERMAN-MERRILL IQ
SIX-DAY SAMPLE, 1947 SURVEY

GIRLS

Terman-Merrill IQ (group centres)

	52	57	62	67	72	77	82	87	92	97	102	107	112	117	122	127	132	137	142	147	152	157	162	167	172	
72																I				I	I	I				4
67															I			I		I	I			I		5
62								I					I	I	I	2	7	2	7	2	2					26
57						I						I	I	2	10	12	5	4	5	2		I				44
52								I	I	5	3	9	10	10	11	6	6			I	I					64
47							I	2	3	4	12	6	10	7	3	I	I			I						51
42							I	I	5	8	18	12	22	4	3	4	I	I								80
37							I	4	7	12	18	11	6	3	5	2										69
32					2	I	5	8	8	15	14	7	4	2	I											67
27				I		I	14	13	15	10	3	2	I													60
22						2	6	6	8	4	2	I	I													30
17			3	I	5	6	6	6	5	I																33
12					2	4	6	I	I	I							I									16
7				I	2	5	I	I	2	I																13
2	I	I	I	5			3	I					I													13
	I	I	5	11	15	44	44	56	61	66	51	50	32	38	33	16	19	8	12	3	5	2	I	0	I	575

In order to make estimates of the mean Terman-Merrill IQ for Scotland, as described in the following section of this chapter, it is necessary to calculate the regression of IQ on verbal score. As inspection of Tables XXIII and XXIV will at once suggest, this is markedly non-linear in both sexes. Quadratics, however, give an excellent fit in both instances. The equation is:

$$Y = \bar{y} + b_1(X - \bar{x}) + b_2(X^2 - \overline{x^2})$$

where x = verbal score; y = IQ; Y is the estimated IQ at given verbal score, X, and given verbal score squared, X^2; $\overline{x^2}$ is the mean of the squares of the verbal scores; and b_1 is the partial regression of y on x at fixed x^2, and b_2 is the partial regression of y on x^2 at fixed x.

The equations for boys and girls respectively (in units of grouping of 5 points: x, 0-4 = 0, 5-9 = 1 . . . ; y, 50-54 = 1, 55-59 = 2 . . .) are as follows:

Boys

$$Y = 11 \cdot 5633 + 0 \cdot 071472(X - 6 \cdot 9651) + 0 \cdot 069039(X^2 - 59 \cdot 905)$$

Girls

$$Y = 10 \cdot 7443 + 0 \cdot 077665(X - 7 \cdot 1391) + 0 \cdot 072605(X^2 - 59 \cdot 991)$$

The fitting of the curves is shown in Table XXV.

TABLE XXV

ANALYSIS OF VARIANCE. REGRESSION OF TERMAN-MERRILL IQ ON VERBAL SCORE

(In units of grouping)

BOYS

Variation of IQ	Degrees of Freedom	Sum of Squares	Mean Square	Variance Ratio
Linear regression	1	5,767·20	5,767·20	—
Curvilinearity	1	405·29	405·29	83·51
Remainder between arrays	12	75·25	6·271	1·29
Within arrays	530	2,572·33	4·853	—
Total	544	8,820·07	—	—

GIRLS

Variation of IQ	Degrees of Freedom	Sum of Squares	Mean Square	Variance Ratio
Linear regression	1	5,786·31	5,786·31	—
Curvilinearity	1	375·26	375·26	81·88
Remainder between arrays	12	49·52	4·127	—
Within arrays	560	2,566·33	4·583	—
Total	574	8,777·42	—	—

That portion of the variation of IQ ascribed to curvilinearity is the difference between the amount due to linear regression and that accounted for by the quadratic function. In both sexes it is a substantial and highly significant contribution, linear regressions giving a very bad fit. The remaining variation between arrays after fitting the quadratics is less than the variation within arrays in the girls and not significantly greater in the boys. In terms of correlation coefficients, the simple correlations of y with x are 0·8086 for the boys and 0·8119 for the girls, whereas the multiple correlations of y with x and x^2 are 0·8366 and 0·8379 respectively. Fig. 6 shows for both sexes (after conversion into units of verbal score and IQ) the mean IQ for each array of verbal score, together with the multiple regression lines.

The sex difference is remarkably large. At the lower end of the distribution boys are five and a half points of IQ higher for a given verbal score, this difference falling off to one and a half points amongst the cleverest children. This should really be stated the other way round: at a given IQ level girls do appreciably better than boys on this verbal test. Although the girls of the 1947 survey are significantly superior to the boys in verbal score, as will be shown immediately, boys are significantly superior in Terman-Merrill IQ. It would seem that at least for present Scottish eleven-year-old children this verbal group test is biased in favour of girls and the Terman-Merrill Revision in favour of boys.

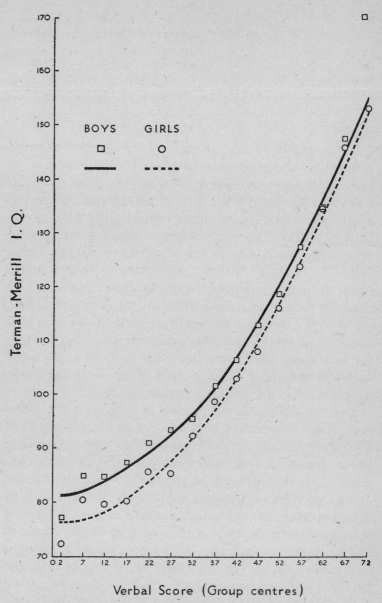

Verbal Score (Group centres)

FIG. 6. 1947 SIX-DAY SAMPLE. MEAN TERMAN-MERRILL IQS FOR ARRAYS
OF VERBAL SCORE, WITH QUADRATIC REGRESSION LINES

THE MEAN TERMAN-MERRILL IQ OF ELEVEN-YEAR-OLD
SCOTTISH CHILDREN: 1947 SURVEY

Table VI (p. 83) and Table VIII (p. 84) show the frequency distributions of verbal scores for the whole age group. These, however, are in units of grouping of ten points. Table XXVI below gives the distributions broken down into five-point groups to correspond with those of Tables XXIII and XXIV.

TABLE XXVI

FREQUENCY DISTRIBUTIONS OF VERBAL SCORES,
in Units of Five Points, for Whole Age Group: 1947 Survey

Score	Frequencies	
	Boys	Girls
70-76	111	90
65-69	638	552
60-64	1,419	1,456
55-59	2,416	2,470
50-54	3,503	3,558
45-49	4,065	4,512
40-44	4,285	4,673
35-39	3,995	4,273
30-34	3,498	3,533
25-29	2,807	2,802
20-24	2,299	2,170
15-19	2,002	1,717
10-14	1,580	1,290
5-9	1,433	903
0-4	1,758	997
Total	35,809	34,996

The equations for boys and girls given on p. 122 may now be used for calculating estimates of the mean IQs for Scotland, the values of X and X^2 in those equations being the means (in units of grouping) as determined from Table XXVI. The estimated mean IQs for boys and girls are respectively 103·68 and 100·75. The use of the quadratic functions instead of the linear regressions alters the figures appreciably, especially the difference between the sexes. Using the linear coefficients, the estimated mean IQs would have been 103·84 and 100·61. It has already been shown in this volume that the method of selection of the six-day sample by date of birth has worked well. The mean age at verbal test of the six-day sample corresponds closely to the mean age at test of the whole age group; hence the use of raw verbal scores does not introduce any appreciable error.

Had linear regression coefficients been used, the sampling variances of the estimated IQs would have been given by the usual formula:

$$V(\overline{Y}) = \frac{\sigma^2}{N} + (\overline{X} - \bar{x})^2 . V(b) + b^2 . V(\overline{X})$$

where σ^2 is the variance of Y at fixed x, N the number tested on both tests, $\overline{X}$ and $\bar{x}$ the means respectively of the whole age group and the six-day sample, and V the variance of the quantity following in brackets. The addition of the second term is due to the fact that allowance must be made for the sampling variance of the slope, since $\overline{X}$ is different from the sample value, $\bar{x}$; the addition of the third term is due to the fact that $\overline{X}$ is not a theoretical value known with accuracy, but has been determined from the data of Table XXVI and so has itself a sampling variance.

As two partial regression coefficients have been used, however, the second and third terms become compound, each being made up of three terms:[1]

$$V(\overline{Y}) =$$
$$\frac{\sigma^2}{N} + (\overline{X} - \bar{x})^2 . V(b_1) + (\overline{X^2} - \overline{x^2})^2 . V(b_2) + 2(\overline{X} - \bar{x})(\overline{X^2} - \overline{x^2}) . \operatorname{Cov}(b_1 b_2)$$
$$+ b_1^2 . V(\overline{X}) + b_2^2 . V(\overline{X^2}) + 2b_1 b_2 . \operatorname{Cov}(\overline{X}\overline{X^2})$$

[1] I am indebted to Mr. P. Armitage of the Medical Research Council's Statistical Research Unit, London School of Hygiene and Tropical Medicine, for this formula.

where b_1 is the partial regression of y on x at fixed x^2, b_2 is the partial regression of y on x^2 at fixed x, and $Cov.$ is the covariance of the quantity following in brackets.

From the data of Tables XXIII, XXIV and XXVI the standard errors of the estimated IQs are found to be ± 0.482 for boys and ± 0.455 for girls. Later in this chapter some further examination is made of the relative magnitudes of the contributions to the sampling variances, as this provides useful information for the planning of further inquiries.

The estimated mean Terman-Merrill IQs of 1947 eleven-year-old Scottish children are therefore:

$$\begin{array}{ll} \text{Boys} & 103{\cdot}68 \pm 0{\cdot}482 \\ \text{Girls} & 100{\cdot}75 \pm 0{\cdot}455 \end{array}$$

There would seem to be every reason for believing that within the limits indicated by the standard errors these are thoroughly reliable estimates. It will be noted that, as already mentioned, the difference between boys and girls is highly significant.

THE RELATION OF VERBAL SCORE AND STANFORD IQ: 1932 SURVEY

The verbal scores and Stanford IQs for the Binet Thousand are given in *The Intelligence of Scottish Children* (p. 92). They are reproduced below in Tables XXVII and XXVIII.

TABLE XXVII
Verbal Score and Stanford IQ
Binet Thousand, 1932 Survey
Boys

Stanford IQ (group centres)

Verbal Score (group centres)	57	62	67	72	77	82	87	92	97	102	107	112	117	122	127	132	137	142	147	152	157	162	Total
72														1			1	1			1		4
67													1	1	1	1	1	3	6	1			15
62							1		2		1		1	2	3	3	1		2		1		17
57						2	2		2		5		2	15	8	1	3	3					43
52						1	5	4	10	12	8	8	4	1									53
47						1	4	4	13	10	13	3	8	6				1					63
42						1	4	8	13	11	14	7	4	1									63
37						1	1	7	11	10	9	6	5	3	2	1							56
32						1	5	12	12	4	10	1	3	3									51
27							3	12	9	11	4	2											41
22					1	5	3	8	3	3	1		1										25
17					2	1	7	6	7	1	1	1											26
12						2	7	4	2	1			1										17
7		1			6	2	3	4	1														17
2	1			1	5	1		1															9
Total	1	1	1	14	14	29	59	58	54	56	48	48	25	37	24	6	5	8	9	1	1	1	500

TABLE XXVIII
Verbal Score and Stanford IQ
Binet Thousand, 1932 Survey
Girls

Stanford IQ (group centres)

Verbal Score (group centres)	57	62	67	72	77	82	87	92	97	102	107	112	117	122	127	132	137	142	147	152	157	162	Total
72																2							2
67									2				1		1	1		1					6
62									1			2	4	1	1		2	1	1				13
57						2	3	5	5	7	5	5	6	2	2								42
52					2	6	2	5	9	5	6	3	5	1									44
47						1	3	5	5	12	12	4	5	1									48
42				2	2	4	9	15	15	11	6	1	1	1		1				1			69
37				1	3	12	12	15	12	9	6	1	1	1		1							74
32					1	3	10	12	11	8	2	3	5										55
27				1	1	10	9	16	6	3	1	1											48
22				2	6	7	6	12	4	1	1												39
17				2	2	11	8	3	1														27
12				3	4	3	6																16
7			1		7	3	1																12
2		2			3																		5
Total	0	0	3	10	22	45	57	69	65	49	49	42	25	24	10	15	7	4	2	1	1	0	500

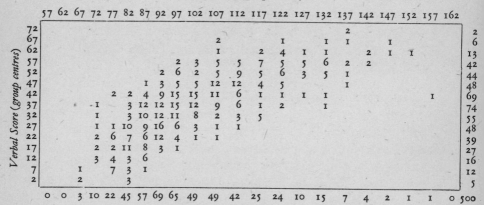

There was some slight bias in the selection of the Binet Thousand, as was discussed at length in *The Intelligence of Scottish Children*, but it does not seem likely that this could make any appreciable difference to the fitting of the regressions. Exactly the same procedure is used as that used above for the six-day sample of 1947. The analysis of variance is shown in Table XXIX.

TABLE XXIX

ANALYSIS OF VARIANCE. REGRESSION OF STANFORD IQ ON VERBAL SCORE
(In units of grouping)

BOYS

Variation of IQ	Degrees of Freedom	Sum of Squares	Mean Square	Variance Ratio
Linear regression	1	3,886·83	3,886·83	—
Curvilinearity	1	160·61	160·61	40·97
Remainder between arrays	12	86·14	7·178	1·83
Within arrays	485	1,901·37	3·920	—
Total	499	6,034·95	—	—

GIRLS

Variation of IQ	Degrees of Freedom	Sum of Squares	Mean Square	Variance Ratio
Linear regression	1	3,011·98	3,011·98	—
Curvilinearity	1	60·48	60·48	14·28
Remainder between arrays	12	37·49	3·124	—
Within arrays	485	2,053·53	4·234	—
Total	499	5,163·48	—	—

As before, there is a highly significant departure from linearity, though the proportion of the variation attributable to curvilinearity is considerably less, especially with the girls. With the girls the quadratic function gives as good a fit as with the 1947 figures, the residual variation between arrays being less than the variation within arrays; with the boys the remainder between arrays just attains the 0·05 level of significance, the largest contribution being due to the lowest array, 0-4 points of verbal score, doubtless a reflection of the fact that the verbal test, if it were to sort out the dullest children efficiently, would have to include negative scores.

The multiple regression equations are as follows:

Boys

$$Y = 10·1900 + 0·038861(X - 38·610) + 0·0019216(X^2 - 1736·9)$$

Girls

$$Y = 9·6380 + 0·072326(X - 37·170) + 0·0013861(X^2 - 1585·3)$$

For a reason which is explained in the following section the verbal scores used are the group central values, 2, 7 . . . . The IQs are in units of grouping; 55-59 = 1, 60-64 = 2 . . . . Fig. 7 shows (in units of verbal score and of IQ) the mean IQs for each array of verbal score, together with the fitted regression lines.

As in 1947 with the Terman-Merrill Revision, for a given Stanford IQ girls do better than boys on the verbal group test, but the difference is considerably less.

THE MEAN STANFORD IQ OF ELEVEN-YEAR-OLD SCOTTISH CHILDREN: 1932 SURVEY

One of the difficulties that arose in 1932, owing to the method by which the Binet Thousand were chosen, was the lack of correspondence between this sample and the whole age group in chronological age at verbal test. As was shown in *The Intelligence of Scottish Children*, however, the ages at verbal test of the Binet Thousand did correspond closely to those of the May-June children. Accordingly estimated IQs were shown in relation to the children born during these two months as well as in relation to the whole age group. For the present estimates it seemed best to use the May-June figures only. It may be possible in a subsequent volume to include a

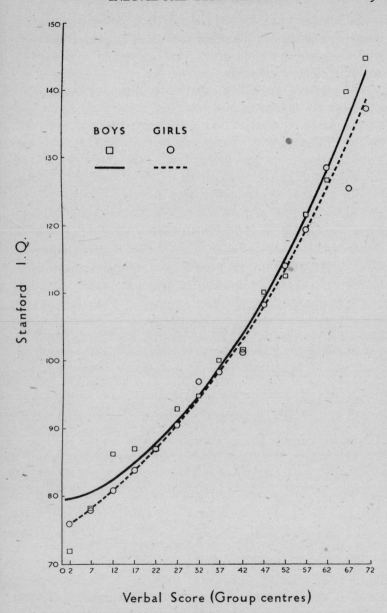

FIG. 7. 1932 BINET THOUSAND. MEAN STANFORD IQs FOR ARRAYS OF
VERBAL SCORE, WITH QUADRATIC REGRESSION LINES

more minute analysis, which may perhaps make use of more information; though, as will be seen from the figures, it seems unlikely that such refinements will make an appreciable difference.

The verbal scores and IQs of the Binet Thousand are available in units of grouping of five points, but the verbal scores for the whole age group in groups of ten points only. It was thought best, however, to use the finer grouping for the Binet Thousand; the calculations have accordingly been made in terms of real units based on the mid-points: for the Binet Thousand, 2, 7, 12 . . .; for the May-June children of the whole age group, 4·5, 14·5 . . ., except that the group centre for 70-76 marks is taken at 72 instead of 74·5. The verbal scores of the May-June children, taken from *The Intelligence of Scottish Children* (p. 62), are shown in Table XXX.

TABLE XXX

FREQUENCY DISTRIBUTIONS OF VERBAL SCORES
in Units of Ten Points, for May-June Children, 1932 Survey

Score	Frequencies	
	Boys	Girls
70-76	17	9
60-69	340	261
50-59	1,191	1,048
40-49	1,836	1,894
30-39	1,849	1,900
20-29	1,268	1,284
10-19	856	830
0-9	608	465
Total	7,965	7,691

Using the equations of the preceding section, the values of X and X^2 being obtained from Table XXX, and using the formula for the sampling variances given on p. 126, the estimated mean Stanford IQs for the (May-June) eleven-year-old Scottish children of 1932 are:

Boys   99·86±0·483
Girls   98·56±0·486

In arriving at the estimates of the means, the method of this chapter is somewhat different from the methods used in *The Intelligence of Scottish Children*. It is interesting to note, however, that the estimates of that volume for the May-June children, using the method considered best (Selection formula (1), pp. 99-100), are almost identical with those of the present section, being 99·9 for boys and 98·5 for girls. The method of the present chapter has the advantage, however, that the standard errors are readily calculable.

Although the numbers individually tested were somewhat fewer in 1932, and although the verbal scores of May-June children only have been used instead of those of the whole age group, the standard errors of the 1932 estimates are not appreciably increased as compared with the standard errors of the estimates of 1947. The increase due to these causes has been cancelled by the narrower dispersion of IQs on the earlier revision of the Binet scale. Actually, the increase in the main sample from about 8000 for each sex to about 35,000 does not reduce the sampling variances by more than about 7 per cent.

As in 1947, boys are superior in performance, but the difference is much smaller and does not quite attain the level of significance.

THE RELATION OF TERMAN-MERRILL IQ AND STANFORD IQ

Appendix I, p. 59, gives results for thirty-nine boys and fifty girls tested on both revisions. The first point to determine is whether there is a sex difference in the relationship of the revisions, or whether, as would be convenient, the whole eighty-nine results can be used for

L

both boys and girls. With ungrouped figures the re-gressions of Stanford IQ on Terman-Merrill IQ turn out to be:

Boys	0·925
Girls	0·831
Difference	0·094±0·062

and estimated Stanford IQ at Terman-Merrill IQ = 100:

Boys	97·68
Girls	96·63
Difference	1·05±1·27

There is no indication, therefore, that boys and girls need be treated separately. The correlation coefficients are: Boys, 0·956; Girls, 0·948: Both Sexes, 0·952.

Small though the numbers are, it seems worth while examining the form of the regression of Stanford IQ on Terman-Merrill IQ, in case there should be some peculiarity. Accordingly, in Table XXXI the IQs on the two revisions are shown, grouped in units of ten points.

TABLE XXXI

EIGHTY-NINE CHILDREN TESTED ON TERMAN-MERRILL AND STANFORD REVISIONS

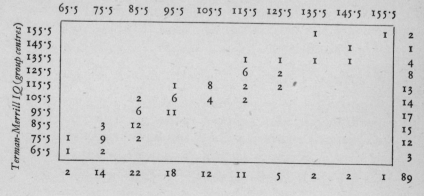

Stanford IQ (group centres)

Terman-Merrill IQ (group centres)	65·5	75·5	85·5	95·5	105·5	115·5	125·5	135·5	145·5	155·5	
155·5								1		1	2
145·5									1		1
135·5						1	1	1	1		4
125·5						6	2				8
115·5				1	8	2	2				13
105·5			2	6	4	2					14
95·5			6	11							17
85·5		3	12								15
75·5	1	9	2								12
65·5	1	2									3
	2	14	22	18	12	11	5	2	2	1	89

REGRESSION OF STANFORD IQ ON TERMAN-MERRILL IQ

(In units of grouping)

Analysis of Variance

Variation of Stanford IQ	Degrees of Freedom	Sum of Squares	Mean Square
Linear regression	1	269·9944	
Remainder between arrays	8	2·8872	0·3609
Within arrays	79	38·8712	0·4920
Total	88	311·7528	—

The residual mean square between arrays is smaller than the mean square within arrays, accordingly there is no indication of any departure from linear regression.

The equation relating Stanford IQ and Terman-Merrill IQ (based on ungrouped figures) is:

$$Y = 97·483 + 0·88167(X - 100·281)$$

where Y is estimated Stanford IQ at Terman-Merrill IQ $= X$. The sampling variance of Y is:

$$V(Y) = \frac{33·859}{89} + 0·00091768(X - 100·281)^2 + (0·88167)^2 . V(X)$$

X being determined from the data and not being a theoretical value.

CONVERSION OF 1947 SURVEY TERMAN-MERRILL IQS INTO ESTIMATED STANFORD IQS AND COMPARISON WITH THE STANFORD ESTIMATES FOR 1932 SURVEY

The estimated mean Terman-Merrill IQs for Scotland, 1947 survey, are:

Boys   103·677±0·4822
Girls   100·747±0·4546

Substituting in the equations of the preceding section, the estimated Stanford IQs for Scotland, 1947, are:

Boys   100·48±0·756
Girls   97·89±0·736

and the final comparison is:

Estimated Stanford IQ—Scotland

			Difference
	1947	1932	1947-1932
Boys	100·48	99·86	+ 0·62±0·90
Girls	97·89	98·56	− 0·67±0·88

Thus the boys show a slight rise, which is smaller than its standard error, while the girls show a fall of almost exactly equal amount, also smaller than its standard error. There is no indication, therefore, that the Binet IQ level in Scotland has changed during the fifteen years; the increase in verbal score has no counterpart in Binet IQ (suggesting that the rise is due to test sophistication); but neither is there any evidence of a decline.

Owing to the high correlation between IQs on the two revisions, the loss of precision through using a different version in 1947 is not as large as might, perhaps, have been expected. Had the Stanford Revision been used in 1947 the standard errors of the differences in mean IQ would have been about 0·65; the sampling variances have in fact been about doubled. As already mentioned, an attempt will be made to improve the estimates, especially by testing more children on both revisions, but it does not seem likely that the conclusion will be altered, namely, that there has been no appreciable change in Binet IQ.

THE PLANNING OF FUTURE SURVEYS

A consideration of the magnitudes of the contributions to the standard errors should prove helpful in the planning of future surveys. As given above, the sampling variance of an estimated mean individual score, when the individually-tested children are a sub-sample of a larger population tested on a group scale, consists of three terms:

$$V(\overline{Y}) = \frac{\sigma^2}{N} + (\overline{X} - \bar{x})^2 . V(b) + b^2 . V(\overline{X})$$

In the calculations on the 1947 and 1932 surveys the second and third terms are compound, but normally linear regression would obtain and they would then be simple. Table XXXII shows for the 1947 and 1932 figures the relative magnitudes of the contributions of the three (compound) terms.

TABLE XXXII

SAMPLING VARIANCES (IN UNITS OF GROUPING) OF ESTIMATED MEAN BINET IQs

	1947		1932	
	Boys	Girls	Boys	Girls
1st term	0·00896	0·00795	0·00800	0·00841
2nd term	0·00004	0·00001	0·00039	0·00023
3rd term	0·00029	0·00030	0·00092	0·00081
Total	0·00929	0·00826	0·00931	0·00945
Standard error	0·0964	0·0909	0·0965	0·0972

The first term depends on the number individually tested and upon the magnitude of the correlation between the two tests. When the sub-sample is truly random, and hence its group-test mean close to the total group-test mean, the second term is negligible, as in 1947. The third term, depending on the number in the total sample, is very small in 1947. Even in 1932, making use of the results for the May-June children only, its contribution does not amount to ten per cent of the total.

If it were desired to detect a difference in Binet IQ between two populations, or in the same area after an interval of time (which was only one of the purposes of the present survey), the most economical procedure would be to use a group test that correlated as highly as possible with the Binet scale, and so to arrange the proportions of pupils group- and individually-tested that the third term became fairly small in comparison with the first. The proportion in the 1932 comparison seems reasonable, that is, about fifteen pupils group-tested for each pupil tested on the Binet scale. It would hardly be worth while increasing the number of pupils group-tested greatly beyond this proportion. An interesting point is that it is quite unnecessary to use the same group test for the different populations; only the individual test need be the same. Thus at successive repetitions the best group test available and one least likely to be familiar in its items to the subjects tested, could be selected. If no group test is employed, the number of children that have to be individually tested in each of the populations in order to detect with reasonable certainty ($P = 0.01$) a difference of one point of Binet IQ would be about 5,300. The incorporation of group testing into the scheme greatly reduces this number—the actual numbers needed could be readily worked out when the group test was selected and its relation to the Binet IQ determined—so that it should be possible with relatively manageable samples to detect quite small changes at intervals of time.

SUMMARY

1. The relation of Binet IQ to verbal score is markedly non-linear, but quadratic functions give an excellent fit. Boys are superior to girls in Binet IQ, the difference in 1947 being highly significant. For a given level of Binet IQ girls do appreciably better than boys in the verbal group test.

2. The quadratic functions may be used for estimating the mean Binet IQ of eleven-year-old Scottish children. The result is:

	Terman-Merrill IQ	Stanford IQ
	1947	1932
Boys	103·68±0·482	99·86±0·483
Girls	100·75±0·455	98·56±0·486

3. A sample of children tested on both revisions of the Binet scale permits the calculation of estimated Stanford

IQs for the age group tested in 1947. The final result of the comparison between the two surveys is:

	Stanford IQ		Difference
	1947	1932	1947-1932
Boys	100·48	99·86	+0·62±0·90
Girls	97·89	98·56	-0·67±0·88

There is thus no indication of any change in the mean Binet IQ of eleven-year-old Scottish children during the fifteen years from 1932 to 1947.

Postscript

It was thought when the computations of this chapter were carried out that of the children tested successively on the two revisions of the Binet scale about half were given the Stanford Revision first and about half the Terman-Merrill. Actually, as shown on pp. 59-60, nearly all were given the Terman-Merrill Revision first and the Stanford subsequently. It might therefore be possible that, owing to practice effect, the Stanford IQs were artificially raised to some slight extent. Any such effect, however, appears to be small. Using figures based on the forty-eight children tested simultaneously on both scales, the estimated change in mean Stanford IQ between 1932 and 1947 is a rise of 0·44 points in boys and a fall of 0·93 in girls. Using figures based on the thirty-six pupils given the Terman-Merrill Revision first and the Stanford subsequently, the corresponding mean changes are a rise of 0·53 points of IQ in boys and a fall of 0·57 in girls. The provisional conclusion, that there is no evidence of any change, is unaltered, but the necessity for investigating on a larger scale the relation of the two revisions is re-emphasized.

IX

THE IMPLICATIONS OF THE 1947 SURVEY

As explained in the Introduction, the major reason for proposing the 1947 survey was to see if the results of a direct inquiry would support the thesis that, in view of the inverse association between measured intelligence and fertility, measured intelligence was likely to decline. Professor Thomson had previously drawn attention to the danger of indirect inferences and had urged that a direct investigation be undertaken, making it possible to compare the performance, in a given intelligence test, of eleven-year-old children at two different points of time.[1] But no one associated with the proposal imagined that the 1947 survey would give a final answer to the question: "Is intelligence falling?" What, rather, was envisaged, was the setting of a precedent—the initiation of the first of a series of surveys which, in the long run, would clarify the relationship between measured intelligence and other factors, and which, when properly interpreted in the light of detailed analysis, might make it possible ultimately to draw a curve of the course of intelligence over time.

EXTENSION OF 1932 SURVEY

Because the 1947 survey was regarded from this point of view, involving the consideration of measured intelligence in its social and economic context, far more information was obtained for the children tested than had been collected in 1932, much of this additional informa-

[1] " The Trend of National Intelligence ", *Eugenics Review*, April 1946, p. 16.

tion being supplied primarily in respect of a sample of ten per cent of the children. It is extremely unlikely that all the information requisite for a full analysis of the various questions was actually specified. Quite apart from the fear of adding another straw to the camel's back, the study of the relationship between measured intelligence and other factors is not sufficiently advanced to enable an investigator to be sure that even the most important data have been covered in a particular inquiry. Progress must necessarily be by successive approximations. But it is one of the merits of a long-term project, that leads suggested by one inquiry can be followed up in the next, that certain aspects can be amplified while others, found to be of little significance, can be discarded.

The 1932 survey asked very few questions in respect of the children tested. The object of the survey was to ascertain the distribution of measured intelligence, and, apart from the tests, the information collected for each child comprised only the name; sex; county, burgh or parish; school; date of birth; and class in school.[1] But, as may be seen from the schedules reproduced in the present report, the 1947 survey went far beyond this. Even the general schedule, to be completed for all pupils, contained seventeen questions, while the schedule used for the ten per cent (thirty-six-day) sample contained twenty-four. The analysis of the answers to these questions will be presented in subsequent reports. It is, however, of some interest to draw attention here, even before the analysis has been completed, to the relevance of the information which has been collected.

RELEVANCE OF SOCIOLOGICAL DATA

We may, in the first place, regard the inquiry as a kind of social survey of children of a specified age, and the questions asked as disclosing the social and other con-

[1] *The Intelligence of Scottish Children*, p. 11.

ditions of those children. Considered from this more restricted point of view, the following tabulations of the data are possible:

1. *The origins and present location of the children.* For each type of area it is possible to distinguish between children born in, or moving since birth to the area in which they were tested. Those not native to the areas in which they now live can also be distinguished by the type of area from which they originally came, and the question of distance of migration can be considered in relation to areas of origin and present residence, as well as to the social status and size of the families to which the children belong. The same kind of analysis can also be applied to school migration—that is, to the number of schools attended by the children up to the age at which they were tested.

2. *School attendance.* This may be an important factor in performance at school and may also influence the test results. The data available will make it possible to analyse the ratio of actual to possible attendance in relation to such factors as type of area, type of school, size of family, and social status. Children suffering from serious physical disabilities can be considered separately.

3. *Evacuation history.* The answers to the relevant questions can be used to give a picture of the extent to which children of this age group were evacuated during the war, considered in relation to such other circumstances as areas of residence and evacuation, and social status of the families to which the children belong.

4. *Housing conditions.* The degree of overcrowding may be shown in relation to family size, social status and type of area of residence. Overcrowding may also be related to the existence of physical disabilities, to school attendance, and to position (i.e. class) of child in school.

5. *Physical conditions of children.* Reference has already been made to these under the previous heading, and under section 2. Further possible relationships may also

be explored—for example, the distribution of height and weight in relation to such factors as family size, social status, over-crowding, school attendance, and position in school.

These headings indicate only the major tabulations possible with the data. As all the information has been transferred to Hollerith cards, it is possible to carry out a much more detailed analysis without any substantial difficulty; in fact, so long as the number of cases in the cell is adequate for the desired degree of accuracy, it is possible to follow up any lead which appears suggestive. This is especially valuable in examining the intercorrelations of series of factors, or in considering the relationship of one variable to the other variables; for example, it is possible to study the influence of overcrowding on school attendance, with such other factors as social class, family size, and type of area held constant. Since even the general sociological schedule, applying to all children who took the group test and to some who did not, contains a substantial amount of information, very detailed analysis of certain questions will be possible.

SIGNIFICANCE OF TEST SCORES

So far, these suggested tabulations have excluded all data relating to the intelligence test, namely, the test scores and the question whether the given child had been previously tested by a group test during the session 1946-7. The inclusion of this information results in much more complex tabulations, but should add to our understanding of the differences in the results of the 1947 and the 1932 surveys, and still more to our knowledge of the factors influencing test results.

One of the difficulties in interpreting the differences between the 1947 and 1932 results is the question of test familiarity. Test motivation also influences results, but there is no reason to believe that, in 1947, children took

the test in a more competitive spirit than they did in
1932. The familiarity factor, however, may well have
changed substantially with the increasing acceptance of
intelligence tests by Scottish educational authorities. At
the same time it is possible that, among the 1947 group
of children, some had already been tested (though on a
different test) within the previous twelve months. On
the first point the survey data do not of themselves throw
light, though it will be possible to compare the group-
test scores for education authorities which have generally
adopted intelligence testing and those which have not.
On the second point, however, the survey itself can provide direct evidence by comparing the results of children
who have, or who have not, taken intelligence tests earlier
in the session, other factors, as far as possible, being held
constant. Similarly, in so far as children given an individual Binet test in 1947 had taken group tests earlier in
the session, it should be possible to compare the relation
between their scores on the Binet test and the 1947 group
test, with the equivalent relationship for children not
previously tested during the session 1946-7. The most
valuable evidence should come from a comparison of the
Binet scores in 1947 and 1932, for the Binet results are
very little affected by familiarity with the test. But this
is by no means as conclusive as it might have been, for
the Terman-Merrill Revision used in 1947 has, as noted
in an earlier chapter, a different threshold, at both the
upper and lower ends of the scale, from that of the
Stanford Revision used in 1932. Double testing of
adequate numbers of boys and girls will, therefore, be
necessary before a comparison of the 1947 and 1932 IQs
is possible, and this work has already begun.

TEST SCORES AND OTHER FACTORS

The complex tabulations of group-test results (and
their translation into IQ units) against other survey data

will be of far greater use in extending our knowledge of the factors at present influencing measured intelligence, and in helping us to plan in a more relevant way future inquiries into this general question. The five main categories of tabulations listed above may, when the test scores are included as a further variable, all be significant in this connection. For example, the crude analysis of test results for urban and rural children would need to be supplemented by an analysis of the results for rural-born children who have moved to urban areas, and for those who have followed the opposite path of migration. For further elucidation of any differences found, it would be desirable to compare equivalent social class groups and, within them, equal family sizes. Type of school, ratio of pupils to teacher, and ratio of actual to possible school attendance, may also be factors which need to be held constant or taken into account. Even this detail may not be entirely adequate unless it can be established—as seems to be indicated—that, for a given family size, position in family is not related to differences in measured intelligence. The 1947 survey, by collecting information on family size and position in family, may throw much light on the latter question. Nevertheless, it is a very difficult question to study. To compare the test scores of children occupying different positions in families of the same size, holding social class constant, may not be sufficient, for these children may really represent different generations. That is, the first child in a five-child family does not necessarily derive from the same generation as the fifth child in another family with the same number of children. Moreover, as neither family may be complete, it is necessary to take into account maternal age, for which information was also collected in the 1947 survey. Consideration of the results analysed in this way may suggest that, at the next inquiry, a somewhat different approach to the question should be taken

—for example, by measuring the intelligence of pairs of sibs taken at random from families of different sizes.[1]

FUTURE SURVEYS

On many aspects of the study of measured intelligence, the full value of the results of the 1947 survey will not, in fact, be extracted until a further survey is carried out. As an example, we may take the apparent paradox of the rise in group scores between 1932 and 1947 and the fall in intelligence suggested by the indirect calculations of Burt, Cattell and Thomson. All of these calculations allowed some environmental contribution to measured intelligence, Thomson going so far as to accept, for the purposes of argument, as much as a fifty per cent contribution from environment, and then concluding that the inference of declining average intelligence was still valid. But this assumes that, at every level of intelligence (or of family size) the proportionate contribution of environment is the same. So far this assumption has not been tested, and, indeed, through lack of available data, could not have been. But another survey at a later date should provide most valuable evidence, for it would make it possible to study IQ changes over time for children belonging to families of different sizes. As there is differential fertility by social class, it would also be necessary to hold social class constant, and it should then be possible to see if environmental improvement (including, of course, better education) had had the same proportional effect upon the IQs of children in families of given sizes but in different social classes.

Another factor which needs to be taken into account in examining the apparent paradox referred to above, is

[1] This suggestion involves substantial difficulties, however, because of the ages of children on which the intelligence test norms are based. It might be preferable—and this, too, has been suggested—to postpone testing the sibs until, in turn, they reach eleven years of age.

changes in fertility. The 1947 survey results show—as have earlier studies—a linear relationship between child IQ and family size, the very low IQs being found in the largest families. Since the relationship is linear, the elimination of the largest families as a result of the general fall in fertility would not affect the tendency to a decline in intelligence, but it might alter the absolute levels at which the decline was taking place. Still more important, of course, is the possibility of a change in the extent, or perhaps even in the nature, of differential fertility. Unfortunately, this is a subject about which only too little is known at present, and we shall have to wait for the results of the Family Census before we can say what trends have been characteristic of Scotland or of Great Britain during the past generation.[1] Such evidence as is now available suggests that social class differences in fertility increased during the nineteenth century but decreased—though to a smaller degree—thereafter. But there are also data for areas in other countries which appear to indicate a positive correlation of fertility and social status, or income, or education. Even if the reversal of differential fertility in the near future seems unlikely, a further narrowing of the gap is not out of the question. The practice of birth control has spread very widely during the past thirty years. At the same time, there is much evidence to suggest that birth control is not generally used completely to prevent the birth of children but rather to control family size. If that is so, then it is possible that the upper economic strata have already reached the lowest level of fertility to which they are likely to fall, while the fertility of the less wealthy sections may continue to decline. This may also apply to the differences in fertility between the more intelligent

[1] The Family Census was a sample fertility census taken in 1946 for the Royal Commission on Population. A preliminary report on the census will be published later in 1949.

and the less intelligent. These speculations imply that, in future, surveys of measured intelligence need more detailed information on certain aspects—for example, data on the education of the parents, and on duration of marriage. The design of such surveys should also be made comparable with that of official fertility censuses, in order that demographic factors may be taken fully into account. In fact, a start has already been made with the 1947 survey, in which social class has been so defined as to permit direct comparability with the Family Census of 1946. In subsequent reports on the 1947 survey, it should thus be possible to pay considerable attention to the influence of demographic factors.

FOLLOW-UP

So far this chapter has been concerned only with the questions bearing upon the analysis and interpretation of the results of the 1947 survey, and with the implications of those results for future studies of the trend of measured intelligence and of the factors affecting it. But the 1947 survey also makes possible a different but no less important line of research—into the factors influencing the way in which individuals possessing various levels of intelligence make use of their intelligence. Since both personal and social factors are of importance here, this kind of research is highly complex. Nevertheless it is of the utmost importance to society to know what happens to individuals with varying degrees of intelligence, and how far obstacles to the full application of that intelligence can be removed by individual or social action.

One study of this nature has already been undertaken. Professor L. M. Terman and his colleagues at Stanford University (California) began in 1921 by sifting the school population of California and obtaining some 1,500 children with IQs above 135. These children have, as far as possible, been followed throughout their lives, and they are still being followed. Both at the initial stage and at subsequent follow-up inquiries, a great deal of information on the physical and psychological traits, interests, background, and life-history of each of the children was obtained, and the analysis of the differences in the degree of achievement of the children, last ascertained in 1945, is both fascinating and of the greatest value.[1] The study is especially valuable, as the authors state, in showing that " although as children all were above the 99th percentile of the generality in IQ, twenty years later they ranged in vocational success all the way from international eminence to semi-skilled labour ", and in attempting to evaluate the factors responsible for the success or failure (in terms of the " extent to which a subject had made use of his superior intellectual ability ") of members of this group of gifted children. Among the factors which appear to be important are background circumstances, such as educational tradition and history of the parents, and parental occupation; and personality characteristics, such as emotional stability, perseverance and social adjustment, which may not, however, be independent of the background circumstances.

The 1947 survey offers an opportunity of undertaking a comparable inquiry in Scotland. In fact, because of the circumstances of the survey, the inquiry might be still more interesting and useful. One of the self-imposed limitations of the California study was that it concerned only children with IQs above 135. But from the point of view of the community it is surely at least as important to know what happens to the generality of children. Another limitation of the California study was the difficulty of obtaining adequate standardisation of some of

[1] L. M. Terman and M. H. Oden, *The Gifted Child Grows Up*. California: Stanford University Press, 1947. For a summary of the results see Lewis Terman, *Psychological Approaches to the Biography of Genius*, Occasional Papers on Eugenics Number Four. London: The Eugenics Society and Hamish Hamilton Medical Books, 1947.

the personality and performance tests applied, because of
lack of an appropriate control group. A follow-up study
deriving from the 1947 survey would be free from both
these limitations. For example, the six-day sample, used
as a basis, would give a truly representative distribution
of intelligence, and could be supplemented by taking, in
addition, further numbers of children randomly selected
from those with very high or very low group-test scores.
Similarly, as the six-day sample is truly representative of
the distribution of intelligence, any other tests applied
to that group would automatically be standardised, and
the results for any sub-sample or supplementary sample
could be compared with the averages and frequency distributions for the group as a whole.

The kind of inquiry suggested would be a difficult one
—more difficult to carry out than the California study,
which naturally appealed to parents who knew that their
children were selected because they were well above
average in intelligence. But every effort should be made to
overcome the difficulties and to profit from this unique
opportunity. Only by undertaking such inquiries can we
discover what use the community makes of its personnel,
and how to ensure that individuals have adequate scope
for employing the abilities they possess.

PUBLICATIONS OF THE SCOTTISH COUNCIL FOR RESEARCH IN EDUCATION

PUBLICATIONS (*continued*)

Official publishers to the Scottish Council for Research in Education
The University of London Press Ltd., Warwick Square,
London, E.C. 4